Reconciling
Theology and Science

Reconciling Theology and Science

A Radical Reformation Perspective

Nancey Murphy

Published by Pandora Press,
Kitchener, Ontario
Co-published with Herald Press,
Scottdale, Pennsylvania/Waterloo, Ontario

Canadian Cataloguing in Publication Data

Murphy, Nancey C.
    Reconciling theology and science : a radical
reformation perspective

Includes bibliographical references and index.
ISBN 0-9698762-4-6

1. Religion and science. I. Title.

BL240.2.M87 1997   261.5'5   C97-931048-2

RECONCILING THEOLOGY AND SCIENCE:
A RADICAL REFORMATION PERSPECTIVE
Copyright © 1997 by Pandora Press,
        Kitchener, Ont. N2H 3C1
        All rights reserved
Co-published with Herald Press,
        Scottdale, Pennsylvania; Waterloo, Ontario
International Standard Book Number: **0-9698762-4-6**
Printed in Canada on acid-free paper
Book and cover design by Clifford Snyder

05 04 03 02 01 00 10 9 8 7 6 5 4 3 2

To
John Howard Yoder

Table of Contents

Author's Preface

I have taught and lectured on the relations between Christian theology and the sciences in a number of contexts. I received my theological training at the Graduate Theological Union (GTU) in Berkeley, California. I had gone there with a Ph.D. in the philosophy of science, having decided that questions about the rationality of Christian belief were more pressing—and more intriguing—than questions about the rationality of science. Shortly after I began my theological studies, Robert J. Russell founded The Center for Theology and the Natural Sciences at the GTU and I became involved in its work.

On completion of my doctorate, I took a teaching position at Fuller Theological Seminary. This has provided further opportunities to pursue questions regarding the relations between theology and science. However, a major shift was required to adapt the work I had done at the GTU for teaching at Fuller. The theological resources at the GTU are Catholic and mainline Protestant, the latter the more liberal segment of the Protestant world. Meanwhile Fuller is evangelical Protestant. At the GTU the task was to convince students that the sciences are relevant to theology. At Fuller, the challenge is to persuade students that theology and science can coexist peacefully.

I describe in chapter six my conversion to the Radical Reformation or Anabaptist tradition. I have gradually come to recognize that the important issues in mainline discussions of theology and science, whether liberal or conservative, are not always the issues of concern to Mennonites, Brethren, and others in the radical tradition. That recognition led to a fruitful collaboration with George F.R. Ellis, a cosmologist in South Africa and a Quaker deeply involved in peace and justice issues there. We asked ourselves the question: What does theology and science look like from a Radical Reformation perspective? Our first attempt at an answer can be found in *On the Moral Nature of the Universe: Theology, Cosmology, and Ethics* (Fortress Press, 1996).

At the time we were completing that book, I was delighted to receive an invitation from Harry Huebner at the Canadian Mennonite Bible College (CMBC) in Winnipeg, Canada, to give the J.J. Thiessen lectures. I agreed to present lectures on theology and science. This would give me an opportunity to test some of these new ideas in a public forum, before an audience from the Radical Reformation community. The present book is based on the four lectures I gave at CMBC in October 1996. I very much enjoyed the opportunity to meet people there, and I thank the publication committee at CMBC for permission to use those lectures in chapters one, two, three, and six.

It has been a delight to work with C. Arnold Snyder and Michael A. King at Pandora Press. I thank them for their courtesy and efficiency.

Francisco J. Ayala made valuable suggestions for improvements; I regret that I have not been able to incorporate all of them.

I want to thank my husband, James Wm. McClendon, Jr. It was in his doctoral seminar on the Radical Reformation that I perceived a call to ally myself with this tradition; I continue to learn from him. I also thank John Howard Yoder for the immense amount I have learned from him about how to understand the New Testament. To him I dedicate this book.

—*Nancey Murphy*
Pasadena, California

Introduction

I describe this book as a Radical Reformation perspective on theology and science. I believe the radical tradition is misunderstood by outsiders more often than are some of the other Christian traditions. Thus it is important to give clues at the outset concerning my understanding of this form of church life.

The Schleitheim Confession (1527), an early attempt to set forth the positions that distinguished the radicals from other Protestants, is still useful (see chapter six). Believers baptism, separation from the world, selection of shepherds (pastors) from within the congregation, and refusal to swear oaths are all calculated to undo the effects of Constantinianism—the identification of the church first with empire, then with nation state, and now with civil society.

Rejection of the sword and adoption of the ban as the most severe form of punishment derive from recognition that God does not use coercion against enemies, and neither may we. Believers baptism and rules concerning reconciliation before breaking bread are aimed at the formation of a community with enough commitment and cohesion to be Jesus' church in the world (at least in its better moments).

Some of my own reflections on radical distinctives: We believe Christianity has primarily to do with real life, here and now. It is only secondarily about life in the hereafter; it is more about changing the world than interpreting its "meaning." Doctrine is important in that it constitutes presuppositions for the way we live.

This realistic and practical attitude toward Christianity absolves us from many controversies over the finer points of doctrine and scriptural interpretation. I shock some Christians by saying I am *in favor* of reading the Bible literally, so long as we begin with the Sermon on the Mount and work our way to other passages after we have gotten that one right.

The question whether the gospel is true does not much arise here. It seems so obviously true to me that the human race would be saved (from itself!) if we would just follow the teaching of Jesus that there does not seem to be much reason to doubt the rest of it.

In the following overview I shall say a few words about how this perspective on Christianity shows up in the chapters that follow.

Chapter one presents a hierarchical model—a schematic representation—to depict the relations between theology and the sciences. Physics, study of the simplest building blocks of reality, goes at the bottom. The rest of the basic sciences (chemistry, the various levels of biology) are located in order above physics, to represent the fact that they study increasingly complex or increasingly comprehensive systems.

Above biology, however, the hierarchy branches, giving place for the physical sciences that study increasingly comprehensive systems. Cosmology comes at the top of this branch since it studies the most encompassing system in the natural world—the entire universe. The second branch includes psychology and the social sciences. I argue that theology can usefully be thought of as the science at the top of the entire diagram since it studies the most comprehensive and complex system of all—God in relation to both the natural world and human society.

The relation between theology and the sciences is much like the relation between one science and another. Each science has its own proper language and concepts and provides a relatively autonomous description of reality. Yet each science can learn from its neighbors. Thus theology provides a relatively autonomous description of reality, yet has some things to learn from the sciences and some things to teach them as well.

However, some will object that classing theology among the sciences is a mistake. Thus in chapter two I argue that theology itself is in fact much like a science. It has its own proper data—from history, revelation, and the cumulative experience of the church. We can think of doctrines as being comparable to theories in the sciences, rationally justified by their ongoing ability to explain the data.

Chapters three through five take up theological issues arising from several of the sciences. In chapter three I consider "boundary questions" that arise in the natural sciences, especially scientific cosmology. I define a boundary question as one that arises at one level of the hierarchy but can only be answered by turning to a higher level. So we will look at ways theology answers questions that arise in but cannot but answered at those scientific levels.

Here are examples. Many scientists say the universe, even time itself, began with the Big Bang. So what happened before the Big Bang? It is not yet clear whether science can address this issue at all. If cosmologists do produce a scientific account of the cause of the Big Bang, then the boundary question is simply pushed back a step.

Another example—and this will be the focus of chapter three—why are cosmological constants apparently "fine-tuned" for life? That is, why do the particular laws of nature that we find in operation in the universe, among all of the countless other possibilities, happen to be among the very narrow range of those resulting in a life-supporting universe?

This is surely one of the most intriguing questions to emerge from recent cosmology. There it has been shown, in calculation after calculation, that if the basic numbers involved in the laws of physics—the strength of the gravitational constant, the ratio between the charges of subatomic particles, and countless others—had been different, even by trivially small amounts, the evolution of the universe from the Big Bang on would have gone quite differently. In almost every case, the resulting universe would be unsuitable for the development of life. It would be too short-lived, too cold, or lacking the heavier elements. In all these countless ways things could have gone wrong from the point of view of the requirements for life—yet they did not. Why?

For that matter, why are there laws of nature at all? Where are they? What is their ontological status? What gives them their force?

None of these questions strictly requires a theological answer, but it is clear enough to people of the Bible that our traditional conception of God and God's purposes answers such questions rather easily. God is the ultimate cause of the universe, whatever that first event may have been. God designed the universe with creatures like us in mind. The laws of nature reflect the will of God for ordering the cosmos.

In chapter four we consider the nature of the human person. There is a deep division in our culture over dualism. Many people, especially Christians, assume humans are made of two parts: a physical body and a nonmaterial mind or soul. Increasingly, though, scientists and philosophers—and biblical scholars as well—are calling this theory into question.

I argue for a non-dualistic account of the person, claiming that such a view is not only more consistent with science than dualism but also more consistent with biblical thought. The "nonreductive physicalist" account I develop also fits nicely in the hierarchical model I describe in chapter one. As we go up the hierarchy of levels from physics and chemistry to biology—from nonliving to living—we do not need to add any new substance such as a vital force. Life is a result of the special *organization* of nonliving matter. Similarly, as we go from the non-human to the human level, no new entity such as a soul or mind needs to be added.

Chapter five deals with evolution. I survey reasons why some Christians opposed the theory. Then I turn to issues that ought to be of special concern to Christians in the Radical Reformation tradition. Perhaps the most important challenge for us is the way evolutionary biology has been used to support an ethic in favor of competition and violence.

In chapter six I address relations between theology and the social sciences. I emphasize the consistency and coherence between theology and the *natural* sciences in the first five chapters, but I believe the social sciences make assumptions about the nature of human beings and their social and political relations that are in serious conflict with the teachings of communities with Radical Reformation roots, including Mennonite, Brethren, and others.

So I have attempted to sketch out in these brief essays a few of the ways in which Christian theology can be reconciled with contemporary science. However, the traffic between theology and science goes in both directions. We sometimes have to correct our theology as science advances. For example, contemporary neuroscience suggests a different view of the person than the one that has prevailed through much of church history.

But sometimes theology must correct science as well. I argue below that this reconciliation is an extremely important task since "evangelistic atheists" in our day are doing an effective job of wedding science to a purely naturalistic worldview. I claim, though, that a worldview involving Christian theology and science is more coherent and has more explanatory power than its atheistic rivals.

Furthermore, for this purpose the theology of our radical heritage offers a number of advantages over mainline accounts. Not all Christian theologies are equally reconcilable with contemporary science. For instance, I point out in chapter three that the question of *how* God acts in the world is central to many theological debates. The view that God intervenes in natural processes, overruling and imposing his will, has been rejected by many Christians. The Radical Reformation tradition affirms that God's action is noncoercive in the human realm; it is consistent to assume that God's action in the natural world is noncoercive as well.

One theological problem that arises in discussions of the nature of the person is the question, what happens to us between death and the general resurrection? Some Christian bodies have affirmed a doctrine of the "intermediate state"—that is, the view that Christians are conscious while awaiting resurrection. However, this doctrine seems to require body-soul dualism so that the soul can be with God while the body decays. Radical Reformation Christians have generally abstained from pronouncements on this issue. Thus this theology will be easier to reconcile with the physicalist account of the person, which agrees with current science.

I claim in chapter five that the practical approach to Christianity found in the Radical tradition leads to a practical approach to reading the Bible. This frees us from the literalism that makes it difficult for some Christians to accept the theory of evolution.

As already mentioned, I believe that it is in the social sciences that we find real conflict with Radical Reformation theology. Some theories here assume an account of human nature that makes violence essential to social life. So the reconciling of theology and science requires dialogue: theology not only needs to learn from the sciences but to speak to them as well. A Radical Reformation perspective may have a crucial word to address to our violence-prone society.

I.

Relating Theology
and the Sciences

1. The Standard Account: Conflict versus Isolation

August 7, 1996: the day scientists announced evidence of primitive life in a rock from Mars. Here in brief is the news. A rock found in Antarctica is shown by analysis of its chemical composition to have come from Mars. Inside the rock, scientists find what appear to be fossils of tiny, one-celled organisms much like bacteria. This has led many to conclude there was primitive life on Mars long ago.

When the news broke, news people asked theologians and religious leaders to comment on theological implications. A variety of reporters questioned me, but I suspect I disappointed them. I'm sure they wanted to talk with someone from a conservative institution like Fuller Seminary because they hoped to get tidbits for the age-old tale of conflict between science and religion.

This story illustrates two common views in our culture about the relation between religion and science. On one side are those who believe that, as science marches on, Christians can always be counted on to object, deny, argue, and ultimately retrench. Because news people favor such accounts, it is easy to think this antagonism is the whole story.

However, my own reaction to the news was typical of at least as many Christians. It simply had not occurred to me that this science story could be theologically interesting. My reaction fit into what Ian Barbour calls the "two worlds" view of science and religion.[1] According to this view, science and religion are so different they cannot possibly conflict. The way the difference is described varies, beginning perhaps with Galileo's quip that the Bible tells us how to go to Heaven, not how the heavens go.

Liberal theology in the modern period has been deeply influenced by the effort to redefine religion to protect it from clashes with science. The effort began with the philosopher Immanuel Kant. He drew a line between science and ethics—pure reason versus practical reason—and concluded that religion belongs to the sphere of ethics and practical reason rather than the realm of science and pure reason. Thus there are two distinct forms of thinking: one is science; the other is religion and ethics. It is illegitimate to argue from one kind of thinking to the other.[2]

At nearly the same time, Friedrich Schleiermacher, founder of modern liberal theology, argued that religion has to do in the first instance with neither science nor ethics—but feeling. So the doctrine of creation, for instance, is not about how or when the universe began but about our awareness of everything's total dependence (here and now) on God.[3] Current expressions of this view distinguish science from religion in terms of facts versus values, meaning, or existential orientation.

I have described this two-worlds view because it is not as familiar as the conflict view. As suggested above, it does not make for good news stories. I hasten to add, though, that the two-worlds view is not my own (despite my temporary lapse on August 7). I am among a small but growing number of scholars who object to both the conflict and two-worlds models.

2. Critique of the Standard Account

I begin with objections to the conflict model. A great myth historians have perpetrated on an unsuspecting public is the "warfare" account of science and religion. Two nineteenth-century authors, John W. Draper and Andrew Dickson White, wrote undeservedly popular books titled *A History of the Conflict between Religion and Science* (1874) and *A History of the Warfare of Science with Theology in Christendom* (1896). Both presented what is now widely recognized as a one-sided account of the history. Looking back, we can see their motives. Draper was "aroused by recent proclamations from Rome declaring papal infallibility and elevating 'revealed doctrine' above the 'human sciences.'"[4] White, first president of Cornell University, was then enmeshed in a conflict with religious folk over the amount of money Cornell was spending on science.

God and Nature: Historical Essays on the Encounter between Christianity and Science, a more recent book edited by David Lindberg and Ronald Numbers, has corrected these biases.[5] Its authors point out that the church, Catholic and Protestant, has often strongly supported science. Some controversies interpreted as church against science are actually much more complex. They may include Christians of one sort fighting Christians of another sort over intellectual issues such as those involved in the shift from the medieval Aristotelian worldview to the modern.

This is not to deny that some Christians oppose certain scientific advances. For example, some conservative North American Christians, convinced evolutionary biology is anti-Christian, are fighting to keep it from being taught in public schools. However, other Christians object to such moves as strenuously as any secular critic. So yes, there are conflicts between religion and science, but they are only a small part of a much more complicated story.

I also object to the two-worlds view of science and religion. There are many cases of interaction between theology and science. If theology and science do interact, then any theory that says they cannot must simply be mistaken.

2.1 Theology and Life on Mars

Consider the Mars rock. Here is a scientific finding that may have a great deal to do with theology. However, the significance for Christians depends on a number of "if's." The first is confirmation that indeed there was life on Mars at one time. If so, then the next important question is whether it arose independently of life on Earth, rather than having been transported from one planet to another.

If life on Mars did arise independently, we begin to see relevance for Christians. The first important issue is the question of how God creates life. As mentioned, Christians remain divided over biological evolution. For Christians who reject evolutionary biology on the grounds of a particular reading of the Genesis creation stories, even primitive Mars life raises theological concerns. A superficial issue arises simply from the fact that Genesis says nothing about God creating bacteria on Mars. "Well," one might reply, "that's true, but there's nothing in Genesis about bacteria, period." In fact, some creationists have long argued that Genesis only intends to tell us about life on Earth, not to say there is no life elsewhere.[6]

Still a theological question remains. Why would a God who created each species individually and deliberately—and this is the main point of difference between creationists and theistic evolutionists—have created these bacteria-like organisms only for them later to die out?

Notice that two-worlds thinkers will be happy with what I have said so far. The Christians who have trouble with science, they say, are those who try to read the Bible as a history or science textbook. However, I argue, against the two-worlds folk, that life on Mars has theological implications for Christians across the board.

The significance for all Christians—whatever their stand on evolution—has to do with what the Mars rock says about whether there are sentient life forms elsewhere in the universe. Until now, experts seem to have been pretty evenly divided. On the one side are those who think conditions for life's origin are so specific and so unlikely to be reproduced elsewhere that we are probably alone. On the other side are those who argue from the vast number of stars that the probability of life arising elsewhere, even in many places, is high.

Simple probability calculations tip the argument in favor of the abundance of life. That is, if life arose independently on two of nine planets in our own solar system, life is probably common throughout the universe. And if there is life at all, then probably there are other advanced forms as well. As far as we can tell, getting the first reproducing organism is the biggest hurdle; once that happens, proliferation and development follow rather easily.

So what if we are not alone? Two theological issues arise for Christians. First (and this is as much an issue for Jews and Muslims), what now are we to make of the teaching of Genesis that the human race is somehow special in God's eyes? Creation in the first account (Gen. 1–2:4a) climaxes with the creation of humans. A disproportionate number of words is dedicated to the creation of humans; it is said that we are created in God's image. The second creation account (Gen. 2:4b-24) again focuses on the human pair and also gives them dominion over other life forms.

There will surely be arguments that life elsewhere in the universe challenges traditional views of the significance of the human race and thus biblical teaching. This will not be the first such challenge. The Copernican revolution displaced us from the center of the universe; subsequent developments in astronomy have revealed how insignificant we are in terms of the size and age of the universe. All this was long before evolutionary biology emphasized our continuity with other species and also, some say, our accidental character. That is, evolutionists speculate that if we could replay evolutionary history, there is no guarantee *Homo sapiens* would appear again.

However, I believe life in other parts of the universe would not contradict biblical teaching on this score. Genesis only says we are special among other earth creatures. What such a discovery would encourage is reflection on why humans, among earth's other life forms, have theological significance. The rest of the Bible testifies that the reason is our capacity for relationship with God. There are many different views about what gives us that capacity, but at a minimum it seems to include the intelligence to permit knowledge of God. There is also whatever makes us social and thus allows for a personal relationship with a "personal" God.

If such relationships are indeed important to God, it would be unsurprising if God's design of the universe allowed for as many relationships as possible. In fact, many ancient and medieval theologians held to the principle of plenitude: the best universe would be one in which all possible forms of being exist. This was their explanation of why we have not just a universe with angels, humans, horses, cats, flowers—but also cockroaches, mosquitoes, and Canadian thistles.

George Coyne, S.J., director of the Vatican Observatory, says, "In the Augustinian tradition [according to which] God is absolute goodness, there is almost a necessity for goodness to reproduce itself, to pour itself out."[7] So it is theologically conceivable for God's creative intentions to include the appearance of other life forms, wherever possible, with comparable intellectual and social capacities.

If this is the case (recall that we now have a long series of "if's"), a further question arises specifically for Christians. What difference would the existence of other intelligent life forms make to traditional Christian claims for the uniqueness of Christ? The Bible tells a story of God graciously reaching out to the human race in all manner of ways and finally in Jesus. It would be inconsistent to assume the existence of other life forms capable of responding to such overtures, yet to reject the possibility of a comparable event on other planets.

There is a principle in theology aptly called "Christological maximalism." This means every possible importance not leading to inconsistency is to be ascribed to Jesus.[8] The varied ways Christians have found to express the significance of Jesus range from "the unique son of God" in John's Gospel and Chalcedonian claims of the "consubstantiality" of Son with Father to more modest views of Jesus as the unsurpassable revelation of God to humankind, or to the even more modest assertion that he is revealer and savior only for Western culture. I emphasize that the hypothesis of other savior-revealer figures in other parts of the universe does not refute strong claims for the significance of Jesus—but will call for reexamination of the language in which those claims are stated.

So the finding of life on Mars shows that neither the conflict nor two-worlds models adequately account for the relations between theology and science. The Mars rock may well call for reevaluation of doctrines regarding Jesus and the significance of humankind in God's eyes. This refutes the two-worlds position that religion and science deal with such different spheres of reality that science and theology cannot interact. We cannot simply say that this scientific discovery conflicts with Christian theology. It probably does conflict with some versions of Christian teaching. But the same finding reinforces other Christian teachings, and in rather surprising ways—such as the teaching about the overflowing goodness of God. Science and religion cannot be isolated. If there are other intelligent beings in the universe, we have to think about what this means for our own and Jesus' redemptive place in God's plans.

3. Theology and Science in Creative Interaction

A third view or model for understanding the relation between Christianity and science is needed. I shall begin working my way toward a better account of the relation between theology and science by considering first relations among the various sciences themselves.

3.1 The Hierarchy of the Sciences

It has long been recognized that the sciences can be organized into a hierarchy, with physics at the bottom, then chemistry, then biology. The rationale is the recognition that physics studies the smallest, most basic constituents of reality. Originally it was supposed that physics studies atoms, but now we have accounts of even more basic particles. Chemistry studies how these subatomic particles are arranged to form atoms and molecules. A tremendous number of chemical phenomena can be explained in terms of physics. Similarly, in biology much of what one learns about cell function, metabolism, and so forth, essentially involves complex chemical reactions. Ultimately tissues, cells, organelles are composed of extremely complex biochemical molecules: proteins, nucleic acids, and so forth.

A contentious issue has been whether psychology can be added to this hierarchy above biology. The rationale for doing so is evident in the suggestion that human behavior—mental illness, for instance—can be understood as an aspect of brain function and especially brain chemistry. Currently there is much interest in genetic explanations of human psychological differences. So it seems reasonable to place psychology in the hierarchy above biology and chemistry. Many sociologists would place their discipline next in the hierarchy and would claim social phenomena can be explained by laws of individual psychology.

Thus we have a hierarchical model for ordering the sciences. Higher sciences permit study of more complex organizations or systems of the entities at the next level down.

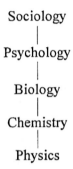

This way of looking at the sciences has a long history. It got its start early in the modern period with the successful explanation of chemical phenomena using the new atomic theory in physics.

While the hierarchical model is well accepted among scientists and philosophers,[9] there has been longstanding debate concerning the issue of *reduction*. The reductionist thesis was promoted most enthusiastically by the logical positivists. This was a group of philosophers, scientists, and others whose views originated in the work of the Vienna Circle of the 1920s and 1930s. One of their aims was the unification of the sciences. This goal was based the hierarchy of the sciences just described.

However, the positivists were interested in a more radical unification of the sciences than mere hierarchical ordering. They wanted to show that each science could be reduced to the one below—that is, that the behavior of entities at a given level could be entirely explained in terms of the operation of its parts, the entities at the next level down. Since physics is at the bottom, ultimately everything was to be understood as a consequence of the laws of physics.[10]

There is no question that reduction was and remains an important research strategy. The behavior of electrons explains chemical bonding, biochemical processes affect human behavior, and so on. But the success of the strategy became a justification for a metaphysic or theory about the nature of reality that creates more problems than it solves. The most obvious problem relates to human freedom. If human behavior is entirely reducible to chemistry, and chemistry to physics, then is it not the case that the laws of physics ultimately determine everything we do and that human free will is an illusion?

However, even as logical positivists were refining and promoting their reductionist program for the sciences, United States philosopher Roy Wood Sellars (1880-1973) was developing a nonreductionist view of the hierarchy of the sciences given such names as "emergent realism," "emergent naturalism," "evolutionary naturalism." A more common term today, and the one I'll use, is *nonreductive physicalism*.[11] Sellars began in 1916 to explicate a conception of the mental as an emergent property in the hierarchy of complex systems.[12] He ultimately developed a conception of nature as forming a nonreducible hierarchy of levels. The levels that Sellars countenances are the inorganic, organic, mental or conscious, social, ethical, and religious or spiritual.

Sellars expressly opposed reductive materialism. According to him, the natural world is one great system, displaying levels of complexity which have emerged over time. He criticized the reductionists for their overly mechanistic and atomistic view of nature. "The ontological imagination," he says, "was stultified at the start by [the picture] of microscopic billiard balls."[13]

In rejecting reductive materialism, Sellars argues that "[o]rganization and wholes are genuinely significant"; they are not mere aggregates of elementary particles. Reductive materialism overemphasizes the "stuff" in contrast to the organization. But matter, he claims, is only a part of nature. "There is energy; there is the fact of pattern; there are all sorts of intimate relations." Thus "Matter, or stuff, needs to be supplemented by terms like integration, pattern, function."[14]

We all know that medium-sized material objects—a desk, for instance—are made up of atoms. One way to make Sellars's point is to raise the question of which is real, the desk or the swirling mass of atoms? The reductionist says only the atoms are real; Sellars says the desk is equally real and must be taken into account in giving an adequate description of the world.

Sellars claimed science and philosophy were in his own day (1932) becoming aware of the principles involved in levels, natural kinds, organization to which the old materialism was blind.[15] Nonetheless, there remain many ardent reductionists, and theirs has been by far the predominant position in philosophy and science to the present. However, I believe the balance is shifting from reductive to nonreductive physicalism, as evidenced by developments in the philosophy of mind as well as science.

Many scientists working at a variety of levels in the hierarchy of the sciences are recognizing this: analysis and reduction are important aspects of scientific enquiry but do not yield a complete or adequate account of the natural world. In simple terms, to understand an entity one has to consider not only its parts but also its interactions with its environment. This means a "top-down" in addition to "bottom-up" analysis is needed. Biochemists recognize that chemical reactions do not work the same in a flask as within a living organism. The science of ecology is based on recognition that organisms function differently in different environments. Thus in general the higher-level system, which is constituted by the entity and its environment, needs to be considered in giving a complete causal account.

Donald T. Campbell, philosopher of biology, describes relations within the hierarchical orders of biology. "All processes at the higher levels are restrained by and act in conformity to the laws of lower levels, including the levels of subatomic physics. Explanation is not complete until these micromechanisms have been specified." But in addition to this reductionistic requirement he adds,

> Description of an intermediate-level phenomenon is not completed by describing its possibility and implementation in lower-level terms. Its presence, prevalence or distribution (all needed for a complete explanation of biological phenomena) will often require reference to laws at a higher level of organization as well. Paraphrasing [the first point] all processes at the lower levels of a hierarchy are restrained by and act in conformity to the laws of the higher levels."[16]

Thus in any science there are many questions that can be answered by reference to factors at the level in question. There are many questions that can only be answered by referring to factors at a lower level. And finally, there are questions that can be answered only by reference to factors described at higher levels of analysis. These latter questions I shall call "boundary questions."

In sum, there have always been objections to a reductionist view, especially in the human sciences. Why else would arguments over nature versus nurture, biology versus environment, proceed? But until recently, the reductionists seemed to have won the day in the natural sciences and were vociferous in the human sciences as well. Now the tide is turning from reductionism, even in the natural sciences. Many now accept that reductionism in science has its limits and that higher levels in the hierarchy have their own causal role to play in the total system of nature.

I shall soon be in position to address the relations between theology and this nonreductive account of the sciences. Before doing so, however, I need to add one refinement to the hierarchy of the sciences. So far, when referring to higher levels I have not made clear whether they pertain to more encompassing wholes (such as ecology as the study of organisms in relation to one another within their natural environment) or to more complex systems. These two criteria usually but not always overlap.

If the hierarchy is taken to be based on more encompassing wholes, then cosmology is the highest science possible in the hierarchy, since it studies the universe as a whole. However, if the hierarchy of the sciences is based on increasing complexity of the systems studied, then the question arises whether a social system is or is not more complex than the abstract account of the cosmos provided by cosmologists.

I believe there is no good way to answer this question. It is therefore helpful to represent the relations among the sciences by means of a branching hierarchy, with the human sciences forming one branch and the natural sciences above biology forming the other. We need to think of the hierarchy of the sciences as rather like a tree: physics, inorganic chemistry, biochemistry, and the various levels of biology form the trunk. One branch completes the natural sciences with cosmology. Another branch contains the human sciences, including psychology and the social sciences.[17]

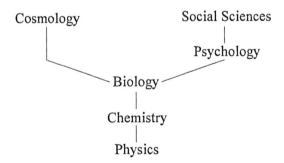

3.2 Theology in the Hierarchy of the Sciences

It is now possible to consider a more radical addition to the hierarchy of the sciences. I have been much influenced in my thinking about theology and science by Arthur Peacocke, an Anglican theologian and biochemist.[18] Peacocke's proposal is that theology should be seen as the science at the top of the hierarchy, since it is the study of the most encompassing system possible—God in relation to everything else that is. This gives us the following picture:

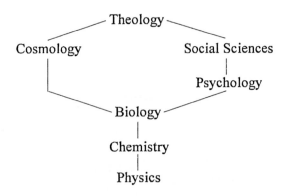

4. Summary

In this chapter I have used a recent scientific discovery (the Mars rock) to illustrate the inadequacy of the two most common views of the relations between theology and science. I have advocated instead the view that theology relates to the sciences in much the same way that one science in the hierarchy relates to another.

Notice how this model reconciles the best insights of both the conflict and two-worlds models. On the one hand, it recognizes with two-worlds theorists that theology and science are truly different. Just as psychology's concerns are different from biology's, so theology has its own proper subject matter—mainly God. It also recognizes that theology and the sciences have different languages. There is no equivalent in biology for psychological terms such as "neurosis" or "ego strength." Similarly there is no scientific equivalent for terms such as "salvation," "grace," and "sin."

On the other hand, this model recognizes, with more conservative proponents of the conflict model, that one cannot isolate theology from the rest of knowledge. Furthermore, just as the neighboring sciences are needed for a thorough explanation, so theology can both learn from and contribute to the sciences.

Consider the theological concept of sin. It can be related to a social concept by saying, for instance, that murder is a sin. But sin cannot be reduced to murder, since sin has intrinsically to do with a person's relation to God. However, social, psychological, and even biological information may be relevant. For instance, do we judge a person a sinner if mentally incompetent?

It is my task in subsequent chapters to exploit this model for relating theology and science. In the next chapter I take up the scientific status of theology itself.

II.

Theology as a Science

1. What Is Theology?

I am intrigued by the question, how do theologians think? My interest arose from the coincidence of several factors in my intellectual development. I began my academic work studying the philosophy of science and concentrating on the question of the kind of *reasoning* involved in justifying scientific theories. While at Berkeley, I encountered atheism for the first time. I had grown up Catholic. I had gone to Catholic schools all my life and even to a Catholic university for undergraduate work.

On Sunday I went to Mass and contemplated the unseen mysteries of the faith. Monday through Friday I spent with people for whom these mysteries were not only unseen—but nonexistent! This raised the question for me of how I could *know* that what I had been taught about God, and grace, and the Holy Spirit was true.

Another factor in my intellectual development was my participation in the charismatic renewal. The interesting thing about a charismatic prayer meeting, from the point of view of a philosopher, is that much of what is described in the Bible is literally visible or audible.

During those years I formulated this question: Does theology or Christian doctrine bear the same relation to the experiences of the Christian life as scientific theories do to the experiences scientists have in their laboratories?" This is a question I have pursued in one way or another ever since.[1]

In this chapter I hope to explain why I give a positive answer and believe it is right to say that theology itself is a science. This will require two steps. First, I will explore the form of reasoning used in science. Second, I will examine more closely the question of what counts as data for theology.

This argument for the scientific status of theology provides crucial support for the model I have proposed for relating theology to the sciences. It would make no sense to count theology as the topmost science in the hierarchy of the sciences were theology itself not a science in any sense or at least very much like a science. That is, we would not think of adding art or music, for instance, to the hierarchy, or even art history. Thus it is necessary to show that theology is a suitable candidate to fill that top spot in the hierarchy of the sciences.

It is nothing new to claim that theology is a science. In the Middle Ages it was viewed not only as a science but as queen of the sciences. This is not a helpful precedent, however, since the very meaning of the word *science* (or *scientia* in Latin) has changed significantly since then, largely due to the rise of modern empirical science.

However, some modern precedents will help. It is interesting to follow changes in theologians' descriptions of theology and theological method and compare them to changing accounts of the nature of scientific reasoning.

2. Parallel Developments in Science and Theology

Philosophy of science is the branch of philosophy that seeks to understand scientific reasoning. Science itself has developed considerably throughout the modern period. But philosophy of science has developed as well and has led to better understanding of how science actually works. At the beginning of the modern era there were two competing accounts of science, which we might call the inductivist and deductivist models. In the twentieth century a more complex account of scientific reasoning was developed, called the "hypothetico-deductive" model. We look at each in turn, along with theological appropriations.

2.1 The Deductive Model

The deductivist view of science was largely consistent with ancient and medieval epistemology, in which geometry was seen as the ideal science. So, just as Euclid had shown that all the theorems of geometry could be deduced from a small set of axioms, the scientists' job was to discover the axioms of physics, or chemistry, or even psychology. From these axioms, all the data relevant to that science should be deducible.

Here is an example of a parallel account of theology. Baptist theologian E.Y. Mullins wrote in 1908,

> I will put my plea in the form of six brief propositions . . . they are self-evident. They are the axioms of religion. . . . These six simple propositions are as six branches from that one trunk of New Testament teaching.

These axioms are as follows:
1. The holy and loving God has a right to be sovereign.
2. All believers have a right to direct access to God.
3. All believers have a right to equal privileges in the church.
4. To be responsible man must be free.
5. A free Church in a free State.
6. Love your neighbor as yourself.

These truths, he says, "are in the moral and religious sphere what axioms are in mathematics."[2]

2.2 The Inductive Model
The competing view of science in the early modern period was Francis Bacon's inductivism. At the beginning of the seventeenth century, Bacon opposed the old medieval conception of a deductive science. He emphasized experiment and observation as the beginning of scientific reasoning. From experiment and observation, scientists were to gather all the instances of the phenomenon under investigation.

For example, if the subject to be studied was heat, the scientist was mentally to gather together all the known instances—sun, fire, blood, and so on. The scientist should also gather a list of negative instances—cool things such as the moon's rays and the blood of dead animals. The positive and negative instances should then be compared so one could form inductive generalizations about what distinguished positive from negative ones.

Bacon's views have been highly influential not only in science but also in theology. For instance, Princeton theologian Charles Hodge wrote in 1871 that the inductive method in theology is so called "because it agrees in everything essential with the inductive method as applied to the natural sciences." Scientists gather and combine facts, being careful to consider all that are relevant. From the facts thus ascertained and classified they derive laws.

Hodge claims that the Bible is to the theologian what nature is to the scientist.

> It is his store-house of facts; and his method of ascertaining what the Bible teaches, is the same as that which the natural philosopher adopts to ascertain what nature teaches. . . . [T]he duty of the Christian theologian is to ascertain, collect, and combine all the facts which God has revealed concerning

himself and our relation to Him. These facts are all in the Bible. . . . [T]he theologian must be guided by the same rules in the collection of facts, as govern the man of science. . . . [I]n theology as in natural science, principles are derived from facts, and not impressed upon them.

So Hodge concludes that it is fundamental to all of science, including theology, that theory is to be determined by facts, and not facts by theory. Just as natural science was a chaos until the principle of induction was employed, so theology is a chaos of human speculations when theologians refuse to apply the same principle to the study of the Word of God.[3]

2.3 The Hypothetico-Deductive Model

An important advance in philosophers' understanding of scientific reasoning in the middle of this century was recognition of hypothetico-deductive reasoning. The term comes from philosophy of science but this is a form of reasoning we use in all aspects of life. Here is a simple example. You come home from work. You find the front door ajar and muddy tracks leading into the kitchen. These are the facts or observations. You form a *hypothesis*: the kids are home. You have not seen them, but you infer that they are there because their presence provides the best *explanation* of the facts you *have* observed.

Note the difference between hypothetical reasoning and induction. The latter would allow you to conclude something like the following: I see muddy tracks in the hall; I see muddy tracks in the kitchen. Probably there are muddy tracks in all the other rooms as well. Hypothetico-deductive reasoning is not aimed at knowledge of *more* tracks but at the *cause* of the tracks—the explanation of how they got there. We can see why this kind of reasoning is called *hypothetical*. We extend our knowledge by inventing hypotheses which, if true, would explain the observed facts.

We have a rough-and-ready sense of what it means to claim that a hypothesis explains a set of observations, but can we make this notion of explanation more precise? One suggestion is the following: a hypothesis can be said to explain a set of observations if statements describing those observations can be inferred *deductively* from the hypothesis (or from the hypothesis along with other premises). This is why philosophers call it hypothetico-*deductive*—to emphasize the role of deduction in relating an explanation to the facts it is supposed to explain.[4]

The discovery by Ignaz Semmelweis of the cause of childbed fever[5] is an example of hypothetico-deductive reasoning. The facts to be explained were statistics regarding the death rates for women in two different maternity wards in the Vienna General Hospital in the 1840s. In the First Maternity Division the death rate for 1844 was 8.2 percent; in 1845 it was 6.8 percent; and in 1846, 11.4 percent. For the same years in the Second Maternity Division the rates were much lower: 2.3 percent, 2.0 percent, and 2.7 percent.

Semmelweis considered various explanations offered at the time. Some he rejected outright as incompatible with well-established facts; others he subjected to tests. One hypothesis was that overcrowding was the cause of death in the First Division. But this suggestion was rejected immediately on grounds that the Second Division was even more crowded.

A second suggestion was based on the fact that medical students practiced in the First Division, while midwives delivered the babies in the Second. The hypothesis was that the higher death rate in the First Division was due to injuries resulting from rough examinations by the medical students. Semmelweis tested this by having the medical students do fewer examinations. The number of deaths did not decline.

A third hypothesis was psychological and based on the fact that the priest who administered the last rites had to pass through the wards of the First Division but not the Second to reach dying patients. The appearance of the priest was thought to have a terrifying and debilitating effect on the patients. Semmelweis tested this hypothesis by persuading the priest to go by a different route so as not to be seen by the women in the First Division. The death rate did not drop.

Finally an accident gave Semmelweis a clue for yet another hypothesis. A colleague received a wound in the hand from the scalpel of a student who was performing an autopsy and died after an illness closely resembling childbed fever. Semmelweis hypothesized that "cadaveric matter" from the scalpel caused the illness and that the same agent, from the hands of the medical students, caused childbed fever. He tested this hypothesis by requiring medical students to wash with a solution of chlorinated lime between autopsies and examinations of women giving birth. The death rate promptly fell to 1.27 percent.

This story nicely illustrates the process of testing competing hypotheses. One asks of each hypothesis, *if* it is true, *then* what other observable effects should follow from it. For example, if the hypothesis about the priest is true, then keeping him out of the wards should reduce the mortality rate. The further observations will either confirm or disconfirm the hypothesis.

Hypothetical reasoning is an indispensable part of science. It is the means by which we expand our knowledge from what we can observe to knowledge of causes—from seen to unseen. Its drawback is that it does not yield the kind of certitude one has in geometry or logic. This is because we can never be sure there is no better explanation of the data than the one(s) we have considered. In the simple example with which I began, it may turn out that the open door and muddy tracks were instead left by a prowler.

3. A Hypothetico-Deductive
Account of Theological Reasoning

The thesis of this chapter is that theology is like science in terms of the form of reasoning it employs—hypothetico-deductive. I intend to show that church doctrines can be construed as *theories* to explain *facts* of the Christian life and that these facts are not so different in status from scientific facts.

Imagine you are a scientific investigator at a charismatic prayer meeting. We have a number of observable phenomena. One of the most striking is what participants call praying in tongues. It sounds like babbling—either spoken or sung. Sometimes one person will speak a message in tongues and another will claim to give an interpretation of it. People prophesy—that is, they speak messages (in English) that they claim have come to them from God. There are often prayers for healings and claims that the prayers have been answered.

These are the unusual phenomena. They occur in the midst of more common Christian practices—singing hymns, reading and commenting on Scripture, praying. There are usually marked changes in people's moods and emotions; they become joyful, sometimes excited, sometimes peaceful. Your job is to explain these phenomena. If you asked participants the cause of the unusual phenomena, they would say it was the Holy Spirit. Gifts of the Spirit empower people to pray in tongues, heal, prophesy. However, observers from the nearby university would probably give a different explanation. They might claim that the unusual phenomena were a result of psychological suggestion. The participants were highly suggestible people and the excitement when they were together produced strange effects. Any healings that took place would be explained as psychosomatic.

So, as in the case of the childbed fever, there is one set of phenomena but competing hypotheses to explain it. Semmelweis asked, "Is it terror induced by the priest or is it cadaveric matter?" We have to ask, "Is is psychological suggestion or the action of the Holy Spirit?"

Just as Semmelweis was interested in ways of ruling out one hypothesis to confirm the other, when I was participant-observer in a prayer group, I was interested in events that would rule out the psychological hypothesis. I was intrigued by participants who claimed to receive instructions from the Holy Spirit before they arrived about scriptural passages to read or other contributions to make. From the variety of comments, all decided on independently, there usually emerged at each meeting a common theme or message. The worship often seemed as well coordinated as if someone had planned it in advance. This could not be explained by group excitement and suggestibility, since the decisions were made at home, prior to the meeting.

I was also interested in apparent answers to prayer. One never knows in a given instance, of course, that a sick person would not have recovered without prayer, or that suggestion had nothing to do with it. Over the course of years, however, the evidence builds up, making it seem less and less likely to be coincidence or suggestion.

So this experience was the source for me of the idea that Christian doctrines are like scientific theories, in that they explain the *experiences* of Christians. Claims about the existence and action of the Holy Spirit form one important part of Christian teaching. I am suggesting this is a part of Christian doctrine susceptible to experiential confirmation. We *need* the hypothesis of the Holy Spirit to *explain* what happens in the Christian life, just as Semmelweis needed the hypothesis of cadaveric matter to explain the death rates in his hospital.

Let me speak more generally now about theology or doctrine. There are a number of interrelated topics about which the church has traditionally taught. These include not only the Holy Spirit but also the trinitarian nature of God, Christology, atonement, salvation and sin, the kingdom of God, creation, the church, eschatology. Two of the theologian's tasks are to propose reformulations of these doctrines and to consider their justification. In this regard, the theologian's task is very much like that of the scientist, who modifies the received theoretical structure and seeks to show its justification relative to the appropriate facts. I do not mean to suggest that all theologians are self-conscious empiricists, although some are. Rather, a "rational reconstruction" of theology is possible, showing that its conclusions (doctrines) *can* be supported by evidence of various sorts.

Let us consider a simplified version of a Christian doctrine to see if it can be understood as a hypothesis that has been developed to explain a set of facts and is rationally supported by its ability to do so. Christian orthodoxy teaches that Christ is both fully human and fully divine. In early New Testament times there was no question of Jesus' humanity; there were still people alive who had known him. However, his divinity could not have been a matter of *observation*, since we know of no observable characteristics of God. Christ's divinity is therefore a kind of theory—something the early Christians could infer about him on the basis of evidence they did have.

I suggest there are at least two kinds of evidence for Christ's divinity. Put differently, there are two sorts of facts this theory explains. These are, first, the church's worship of Christ and obedience to him as absolute Lord; and second, Jesus' own claims about himself.

New Testament evidence suggests that worship of Jesus began early in Christian history. For instance Philippians 2:5-11 is taken by scholars to be a pre-Pauline hymn. If it is, then this shows that Jesus' claim to Christian worship was recognized even before the date of that letter. The hymn proclaims that "at the name of Jesus every knee should bow—in heaven, on earth, and in the depths—and every tongue acclaim 'Jesus Christ is Lord,' to the glory of God the Father" (Phil. 5:10-11 REB).

However, it is only *later* that Jesus is specifically referred to as divine. For example, consider Titus 2:13, "looking forward to the happy fulfillment of our hope when the splendor of our great God and Saviour, Christ Jesus will appear" (REB). We can assume that the practice of worshiping Christ, especially in a Jewish monotheistic setting, called for an *explanation*. In that setting it is difficult to imagine a suitable explanation other than the identification of Jesus with God.

A related sort of evidence for Jesus' divinity is the fact that his moral teaching was accepted as authoritative. Jesus made ultimate claims on his disciples' obedience, and the community recognized his legitimate lordship over them. The early Christian community's practice of taking Jesus' word as the last word in ethical matters cries out for explanation, and again this explanation involves identification of the Lord Jesus with Israel's Lord, Yahweh.

My second category of evidence is Jesus' own claims and actions. It is questionable whether Jesus ever referred to himself as divine.

However, he is pictured in the Gospels as acting and speaking in ways that would be outrageous if he were not. In fact, many of his utterances were apparently considered blasphemous by his contemporaries. Consider these examples:

First, Jesus called God *Abba*. Some say this is equivalent to calling God "Daddy" or "Papa" (e.g. Mark 14:36).

Second, Jesus placed himself above God's law. For instance he says, "You have heard that it was said to those of ancient times, 'You shall not murder'; and 'Whoever murders shall be liable to judgment.' But I say to you that if you are angry with a brother or sister, you will be liable to judgment. . ." (Matt. 5:21).

Third, Jesus claimed that all will be judged on the basis of their response to him. "And I tell you, everyone who acknowledges me before others, the Son of Man also will acknowledge before the angels of God..." (Luke 12:8; cf. Matt. 25:31-46).

Now if Jesus had been condemned to death, particularly for blasphemy, and that had simply been the end of him, we might agree with his Gospel accusers. However, Christians early and late have seen the resurrection as evidence of God's vindication of Jesus. And what could better excuse him from the charge of blasphemy than the actual possession of equality with God? These ideas converge in Romans 1:4, where Paul says that Jesus is "declared to be Son of God with power according to the spirit of holiness by resurrection from the dead."

In sum, if we ask what *theory* about Jesus could rightly account for this collection of facts, including his own outrageous behavior, his resurrection, his followers' obedience and even worship, one hypothesis from which all of these facts would follow is that of his divinity. Here we see the same kind of development as we do in science. We reason from things we know (Jesus' behavior, the practices of the early church) to hypotheses about unobservable states of affairs (in this case, Jesus' divinity). As the evidence accumulates, and competing hypotheses are ruled out, our confidence grows to the point where we can legitimately say we have knowledge of these unseen realities.

Now there are sure to be several objections to what I have said so far. The first is that scientific knowledge is not certain knowledge. We have to be wary of new developments coming along in the future. To call theological claims such as the divinity of Christ or the existence of the Holy Spirit hypotheses or theories is to say they are uncertain, open to development. This sounds like heresy.

My response is that in science, while we never claim absolute certainty, there are varying degrees of confidence. For example, no one really believes the law of gravity is going to be overturned in the future. However, there are extremely abstract and speculative theories in science as well. For instance, there is Stephen Hawking's theory that the universe has no beginning because time loses its directionality as we go back toward the Big Bang. Theologians recognize the same sort of variation in Christian teaching. There are the basics about God and Jesus and salvation that we cannot imagine ever being given up. But there are also a variety of more speculative theories, such as different accounts of the relations among the persons of the Trinity and debates over such questions as whether God is eternal or timeless.

In my example I suggested that the theory of the divinity of Christ is based on two kinds of data: The moral life and worship of the church are both forms of church *practice*; Jesus' sayings and resurrection are both *historical events*.

A second objection might then be that neither of these categories of fact provides a suitable starting point for a scientific theology. After all, we are seeking the data, the "given." There has been an intense debate concerning the resurrection throughout the modern period; some claim that it could not be an historical event or that we could not know that it happened.[6] There is also a continuing quest among scholars to distinguish between the authentic sayings of Jesus and other statements put into his mouth by the early church.[7] So neither of the historical facts I have adduced is a simple given.

Nor are the practices of the church given, yet this is in a different sense. They are not given but made. One might ask, then, how such practices could have consequences for theology. Are they not arbitrary? How can they tell us anything *about God*?

Objections to both sorts of data can be answered in a way consistent with the best current understanding of data in science. Philosophers of science have come to recognize that scientific data are the product of selection, interpretation, and complex procedures involving significant theoretical components. Etymologically, *fact* is a more appropriate term than *datum*. This is because the underlying meaning conveyed by the term *fact* includes the suggestion that facts, although not mere fabrications, are in some sense *made*, not simply *given* to experience.

For example, in the debate over the Copernican theory of planetary motion, it was necessary to supply a theory of optics to explain why appearances through this new instrument called a telescope should be trusted as data for astronomy. How is one to know that these are not illusions produced by the new technology? Or consider a more homely example: a temperature reading seems to be a very straightforward sort of fact. However, construction of a thermometer and explanation of why its readings should be significant requires a great deal of theory about heat transfer, expansion, and so forth. In science, these theories are called "theories of instrumentation."

Similarly, the crucial events of the life of Jesus and of the earliest years of the church can only be reconstructed for today's theologian by means of theories. Since the texts are the primary sources, most of the theories involved here are theories not of instrumentation but of *interpretation*. The reasoning from text to interpretation is as complicated as the reasoning from interpretation to theology. Thus the theologian's data may be the biblical scholar's theory. But this complication nicely parallels the situation in science.

Now recall the objection I mentioned above to the use of church practices as data for theology. They appear to be arbitrary, and it is not clear how they can tell us anything about God. This case, too, is analogous to the one in astronomy. There a *theory* was needed to explain why appearances through the eye piece of a strange new instrument could be trusted to yield information about the nature of the heavenly bodies. I call the needed theological hypothesis the theory of Christian discernment. This theory asserts that the Christian community, in virtue of the presence of the Holy Spirit, has the ability to judge whether or not practices, teachings, and prophecies are of the Spirit of Jesus. Christians possess an *inner witness* regarding what is or is not of God, as well as *public criteria* to test these judgments. In the New Testament this was often referred to as testing or discerning the spirits.

Although the theory of discernment has received less attention than its due in recent years, it has not disappeared from the Christian scene. The sixteenth-century Anabaptists, as well as some of their contemporary descendants, place great emphasis on communal judgment. Their criteria include consistency with Scripture and consensus of the community, on the assumption that the teachings and directions of the Holy Spirit cannot be self-contradictory.

The most noted theological investigation of discernment is that of Jonathan Edwards, the eighteenth-century Calvinist. Edwards wrote extensively about the signs of a work of the Spirit of God. He emphasized changes in the character of those genuinely converted, especially manifestations of the fruits of the Spirit.[8]

A particularly important aspect of Edwards' work was his account of why the fruits of the Spirit, especially love, should be criteria of a work of God. In brief, the Holy Spirit is the Spirit of God, and God's very nature is love. Thus love manifested in the convert's life is evidence of the presence and action of God himself. So Christian discernment criteria are a consequence of the Christian doctrine of God.

To return to the objections raised above, church practices may indeed be arbitrary, but they should not be; the church has been charged with the task of testing the spirits to see whether they are of God. When such admittedly fallible discriminations are made, the church and its theologians have a growing knowledge of God based upon memory of God's words and deeds in human history. These words and deeds, recorded in Scripture and in the collective memory of the church, serve the same function for theologians as experimental results do for scientists.

4. Objectivity versus Subjectivity

It is common in our culture to contrast science and theology or religion. Science is said to be objective, based on facts, able to prove its conclusions. Religious belief is just that—belief. Religious beliefs are subjective, based on personal values. My emphasis above is on the extent to which theological claims can stand up to the same sort of rational scrutiny as scientific theories.

Along the way, we have also seen a change in views of science. It was only in the earliest days of science that anyone believed that scientific theories could be proved. *Proof* is a strong word, now recognized to be at home only in formal systems, such as logic and mathematics. Scientific theories admit of varying degrees of *confirmation*—not proof.

In the past generation further developments in philosophy of science and the sociology of science have made it clear that science is actually more like theology than many have assumed. Thomas Kuhn has examined revolutions in science, such as the change from medieval Aristotelian physics to modern physics, best exemplified in the work of Isaac Newton, then from Newtonian physics to relativity theory.[9]

Kuhn emphasizes the role of authoritative texts guiding each of these scientific "paradigms"—which sounds a bit like Scripture. He emphasizes the importance of a community of scholars who only question "the basics" in their field during rare revolutionary periods—which sounds a bit like church history with its intermittent reformations. He stresses the way theoretical understanding shapes the scientists' experience, and how they have to be trained in the scientific tradition to participate in scientific practices—which sounds a bit like Christian formation.

So while it is clear that there are significant differences between theology and the natural sciences—it is indeed easier to get clear-cut results in physics and chemistry than in theology—the contrasts are not as sharp as many suppose. Both theology and science are the result of the human quest for understanding. Both have phenomena (data) to which they must be faithful. In both cases, rigorous thinking is required. But we must remember the fallible, historically conditioned character of both enterprises. Both provide genuine knowledge, but it is *human* knowledge nonetheless.

5. Summary

It is time to sum up. In chapter one I proposed a model for relating theology to a branching hierarchy of the sciences. I placed theology at the top of that hierarchy, claiming that it is the most encompassing of all the sciences in that it studies the relations between God and the entire universe.

My purpose in this chapter has been to show that theology is enough like a science to warrant its being placed in such a relation to the other sciences. To do so, I have considered the kind of reasoning scientists use—hypothetico-deductive reasoning—and have tried to show that theologians use exactly the same methods. I paid some attention to the sorts of facts theologians have at their disposal. These include Christian experience, church practices, historical events—many of them recorded in Scripture.

I noted that some would raise objections to use of data of this sort. These certainly are not the sorts of data physicists would use. But then, the data used in biology are not the same as those in physics. And sociologists and psychologists use different kinds of data than cosmologists. Each science has its own kinds of data.

An interesting fact about data, only recently recognized by philosophers of science, is that part of the theoretical structure of each level in the hierarchy provides a justification for the use of its data; in science we call these theories of instrumentation. For theologians, there is a crucial theory—that of revelation or inspiration—that explains why biblical texts count as data. I also mentioned in this regard the theory of discernment, explaining why the judgments church members make together in prayer should be expected to tell us something about the will of God and not merely about the church.

In the next chapter I argue that the fine-tuning of the cosmological constants provides evidence for the doctrine of creation. So we also have to keep in mind that, just as the natural sciences draw support from neighboring sciences, so too theology draws support from levels below. In the final chapter I shall make the bolder claim that theology can and should correct some of the theories at the levels below.

III

Cosmological Fine-Tuning
and Design

When I look at your heavens, the work of your fingers,
the moon and the stars that you have established;
What are human beings that you are mindful of them,
mortals that you care for them? —*Psalm 8:3-4*

Thus says the LORD, the creator of the heavens, he who is
God, who made the earth and fashioned it and by himself fixed it
firmly, who created it not as a formless waste but as a place to
be lived in: I am the LORD, and there is none other. —*Isaiah*
45:18 (REB)

1. Divine Action—The Critical Issue

Some readers might be surprised to learn that one of the world's oldest
astronomical institutes was established by the Vatican. The Vatican
Observatory, approximately 100 years old, is based in the Pope's
summer palace on a mountainside outside of Rome. Several years ago
Pope John Paul II made a request to the Vatican Observatory to include
in its research program an investigation of possible relations between
theology and science. I had the good fortune to be asked to help plan the
work they would sponsor.

The planning group to which I belong proposed that the
Observatory sponsor a series of conferences on the topic of God's action
in the world in light of current developments in science. There were a
number of reasons for this choice of topics. First, it seems the question
of how God acts in the world is at the heart of many of the conflicts, both
real and perceived, between science and Christianity. For example, North
American creationist controversies are at base a conflict over *how* God
creates.

Second, different views of divine action have had a great deal to do
with creating the differences between liberal and conservative views of
theology.[1]

Finally, this is the point at which modern science has had its
greatest impact on theology in the modern period. To tell the story

briefly, when Newton's Laws came to be seen as a complete account of all the movements of matter in the universe, the question arose, what is left for God to do?

But science itself has changed dramatically since the days of Newton. It seemed the proper time to investigate what difference these scientific changes would make to this crucial theological and philosophical issue.

We proposed a series of five conferences, each dealing with a different aspect of contemporary science. The first conference dealt with quantum cosmology and with what has been called the fine-tuning of the universe. The second addressed the new science called chaos theory. The third focused on biological evolution.[2] In the future, we take up neuroscience and quantum theory.

In this chapter I pursue the subject matter of that first conference, the apparent "fine-tuning" of cosmological constants. What this involves is a recognition that, as one astronomer put it, *the universe looks as though it knew we were coming*. Assorted results in cosmology have brought scientists, even those with no prior interest in Christianity, to consider the hypothesis that the universe was designed specifically, in Isaiah's words, as "a place to be lived in" for beings like ourselves.

2. Cosmological Fine-Tuning

I begin with background on current scientific cosmology. The current state of the universe can best be explained by assuming an initial event, called the Big Bang, between 10 and 20 billion years ago. As the term *Big Bang* suggests, this was like a huge explosion. The universe has been expanding—actually flying off in all directions at a terrific speed—and cooling ever since.

In the earliest stages, the "stuff" of the universe was not yet differentiated into matter and energy. Later, atoms of the lightest gases formed. Stars congealed from clouds of gas between one and five billion years into the universe's history. The heat and pressure inside stars allowed for the "cooking" of the heavier elements, such as carbon. At a certain stage in their development the stars explode and in this way the heavier elements are distributed throughout the universe. These heavy elements are necessary to provide the materials for planets and, ultimately, for living beings.

Calculations show that a number of factors early in the history of the universe had to be adjusted in a remarkably precise way for the process to result in a habitable universe. One factor is the mass of the universe—the total amount of stuff in it. In addition there are the four basic forces: gravitation, electromagnetism, and the strong and weak nuclear forces.

Two of these forces are familiar in everyday life: gravity, of course, and electromagnetism. The latter has made a great impact on modern life in that it is the basis for electric motors. Of course it has had a large role to play in the universe long before we learned how to harness it. Electromagnetism is the force responsible for atomic structure and chemical reactions. The strong and weak nuclear forces, as the terms suggest, are active within the nuclei of atoms; we have come to know about them, practically speaking, from nuclear energy and nuclear bombs. Besides these four forces, some other important numbers are the ratios of the *masses* and *charges* of various subatomic particles to one another.

Calculations show that if any of these numbers had been much different, even by a small amount, the universe would not have turned out to be a place in which intelligent life of any sort could exist. Life requires a universe with a sufficient time span. It requires the existence of elements heavier than the gasses that constituted it in the beginning. It requires stars and planets. In countless ways things could have gone wrong, leaving it, in Isaiah's words, "a formless waste."

The following are a few examples of the fine-tuning that was required. The density of matter in the universe is a critical factor. Recall that the universe is still expanding after the Big Bang and also that gravitational attraction depends on the *masses* of the bodies being attracted. If the total mass of the universe were much greater, gravitational attraction would too easily overcome the expansive force resulting from the initial explosion. This would mean that the universe's expansion would first slow, then reverse. Finally the whole universe would collapse into a tiny point—before stars, planets, and life had a chance to form. Scientists call such an event the Big Crunch. And, of course, if the force of gravity itself were stronger, the same result could be expected.

On the other hand, if the mass were much smaller, then the universe would spread out and cool off too quickly. The gases have to be dense enough to form stars and then later planets in order for life to have a chance to develop.

Carbon is one of the basic elements needed for life; many of the calculations have to do with necessary conditions for its formation inside stars and its later distribution throughout the universe. It can be shown that if the nuclear strong force were either 1 percent weaker or 1 percent stronger, carbon would not form within the stellar ovens. In fact it has been calculated that the strong force had to be within .8 and 1.2 times its actual strength for there to be any elements at all with atomic weights greater than 4.

The nuclear weak force's very weakness allows our sun to burn gently for billions of years rather than blow up like a bomb. Had this force been appreciably stronger, stars of this sort would be impossible. But if it were much weaker the universe would be composed entirely of helium.

Finally, if electromagnetism had been stronger, stars would never explode and the heavier elements needed for life would not be available.

Here are some remarkable numbers. The ratio of the strength of electromagnetism to the strength of gravity appears to be crucial. Changes in either force by as little as one part in ten to the fortieth power (that is, ten followed by forty zeros) would spell catastrophe for stars like our sun. Electrons and protons have equal but opposite charges. It has been estimated that a charge difference of more than one part in 10 billion would mean that there could be no macroscopic objects; that is, there could be no solid objects weighing more than about a gram.

The ratio between gravity and the nuclear weak force may have to be adjusted as accurately as one part in ten to the 100th power to avoid either a swift collapse of the universe or an explosion.

Cosmologists began noting these strange coincidences in the 1950s. By now several books have appeared with page after page of such conclusions.[3] What are we to make of these results?

3. A Theological Interpretation?

In chapter one I proposed a model for understanding the relations between science and theology that begins with the old positivist notion of the hierarchy of the sciences. According to this model, the sciences can be organized in order according to the complexity or comprehensiveness of the systems they study. Because of this ambiguity—complexity versus comprehensiveness—I suggested a branching hierarchy and located the natural sciences above biology on one branch and the human sciences on the other.

However, I rejected the view that the laws of physics somehow determine everything else. I proposed instead a view called nonreductive physicalism. This view attributes equal *reality* to the entities studied by each of the sciences—for example, desks are just as *real* as electrons; social structures are just as *real* as individuals. It also recognizes top-down explanation; that is, a question may arise in the science at one level that can only be answered by referring to realities at a higher level. I called these questions "boundary questions."

I suggest that this so-called fine-tuning of the cosmological constants is just such a question. As far as we can tell at present, scientific cosmology itself can *describe* this phenomenon, this remarkable set of coincidences, but cannot *explain* it. It seems to call for an explanation of a different kind or level. From a Christian perspective the ideal explanation, of course, is divine creation. That is, if we accept the proposal I made in chapter one to place theology at the top of the hierarchy, it is natural to move directly to a theological explanation.

3.1 Evidence for the Existence of God?

I begin by emphasizing that the fine-tuning should not be expected to *prove* the existence of God. I shall claim, rather, that it adds weight to other arguments coming from more traditional sources; it provides an important further sort of *confirmation* for God's existence and creative role.

Let us review how evidence works in science before proceeding to the question of how the fine-tuning provides evidence for creation of the universe by God. Recall that there was a long debate in the history of science whether scientific reasoning was mainly deductive, as in geometry, or whether it was merely the drawing of inductive generalizations from observations.

An important advance in more recent philosophy of science was the recognition of what has come to be called hypothetico-deductive reasoning. Philosophers now agree that scientific theories are neither mere inductive generalizations from facts nor deductive consequences of first principles. In the first instance they are free inventions of the imagination—hypotheses. However, these hypotheses are then tested by showing that scientific facts follow from them deductively.

The problem with hypothetico-deductive reasoning is that one can usually invent more than one hypothesis to explain any set of data. This is the reason that, however well-confirmed a theory may be, scientific knowledge never reaches the level of certainty we have in mathematics or logic.

This factor is important to keep in mind in science; scientific theories always face the danger that some young Einstein will come along and provide a new and better alternative. It is also important to remember this when assessing any arguments for the existence of God that depend on empirical evidence.

3.2 William Paley's Design Argument

The most famous such argument was William Paley's at the beginning of the nineteenth century.[4] He argued that if he found a stone on the heath and were asked how it came to be there, he might answer that

> for any thing I knew to the contrary, it had lain there forever; nor would it perhaps be very easy to show the absurdity of this answer. But suppose I had found a watch upon the ground, and it should be enquired how the watch happened to be in that place, I should hardly think of the answer which I had before given, that, for anything I knew, the watch might have always been there. Yet why should not this answer serve for the watch, as well as for the stone?

Paley answered, "For this reason, and for no other, viz. that when we come to inspect the watch, we perceive (what we could not discover in the stone) that its several parts are framed and put together for a purpose."[5]

The universe, Paley claimed, is like a watch. For his evidence he turned mainly to anatomy for examples of body parts perfectly adapted to serve their functions. His conclusion was that there must be a divine mind, whose goodness is shown by the fact that we have been created with the capacity for pleasure. And such an intelligent, benevolent creator must be expected to reveal himself to his creatures.

We can construe Paley's argument as hypothetico-deductive in form. The fact or observation to be explained is the order in the world—in particular the remarkable fitness of biological organs for their purposes and the fitness of organisms to their environments. What theory or hypothesis, if true, could possibly explain all this? To Paley, it seemed that only the hypothesis of an intelligent, benevolent creator would do.

One reason some Christians objected to Darwinian evolution was that it spoiled this popular apologetic argument. In effect, Darwin proposed a *competing hypothesis* to explain biological adaptation: a combination of random variation with natural selection.

But long before Darwin, and shortly *before* Paley published his own book, the philosopher David Hume had pointed out the vulnerability of arguments like Paley's—there are alternative hypotheses. First, the universe shows a great deal of order, but there is disorder and evil as well. So how can we know that it was created by one all-good God?

Perhaps it was created instead by a team of juvenile or superannuated deities working together. Perhaps the universe is more like an organism than a watch and was produced by propagation. Or perhaps it is merely a fortuitous arrangement of atoms.[6]

3.3 Fine-Tuning and Design

It is one of the ironies of history that Darwinian evolution was seen as the final blow to Paley's design argument (despite Hume's earlier critiques). Yet evolutionary biology is itself an important contributor to the new scientific knowledge that seems, once again, to call for a theory of divine design. This is because the fine-tuning arguments themselves all depend on asking the question, what conditions need to be fulfilled in the universe to allow life to *evolve?*

So what are we to make of the fine-tuning? There is wide agreement that it needs *some* sort of explanation. Can we conclude that the explanation must be that it is the work of the Christian God, or would this argument be subject to the same sorts of criticisms that Hume had already raised, 200 years ago?

The important question to investigate first is whether there are scientific explanations of the fine-tuning. Recall my picture of the relation between theology and science, and especially between theology and cosmology:

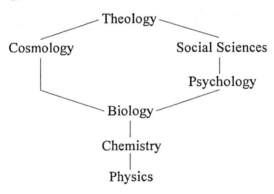

Can we claim to have found a question that cannot be answered at the cosmological level alone—that is, a boundary question? Or is this just a new puzzle for cosmology itself to answer? This is a contested issue.

In fact a variety of nontheistic hypotheses have been proposed, either to explain the fine-tuning or else to try to explain *away* our sense that it needs explaining. Here are four of the competing hypotheses. First, the "anthropic principle"; second, pure chance; third, mathematical (or logical) necessity; and fourth, many universes. I shall explain each briefly.[7]

The first approach claims it is a simple mistake to be surprised that the universe is suited to life; there is nothing to explain. The universe cannot be observed without observers. Thus of course any universe that contains observers must be one that permits life.[8]

The second suggestion is that yes, it is amazing that the universe should have turned out to be life-supporting, but this is just a matter of chance. There is nothing more to be said. This claim can be taken in either of two ways. It might be taken as a statement about the limits of our knowledge. This is just the way the universe happens to be and there is no further explanation. (This sounds like Hume's "fortuitous arrangement of atoms.")

However, some authors make it sound as though the chance hypothesis is a sort of metaphysical claim. They state or imply that Chance, with a capital "C," is somehow the ultimate principle behind reality. In either case, we have a meta-scientific claim, a claim above the power of science independently to confirm.

Another suggestion is that it will someday be shown that there is only one set of numbers that solve the equations comprising the basic laws of nature. If so, this would, in a sense, provide a scientific explanation for the fine-tuning of the individual constants, masses, and other quantities. It would provide no ultimate explanation, however, because we still can wonder at the coincidence that the only possible universe is also life-supporting and at the fact that this one-and-only possibility exists at all. We are back to the old question of why there is something rather than nothing.

A natural move to explain the fine-tuning (or to explain it away) is to propose that we are in but one of vastly many universes. This might be because there is a very long or infinite series of universes. After an initial Big Bang a universe develops, then finally the expansion ceases, gravitational attraction pulls it back together, and there is a Big Crunch. After this comes another Big Bang, and so on indefinitely.

This explanation requires an additional assumption—for some reason all of the universes in this series are different. This assumption would allow for random variation of the cosmological constants. By chance, then, one or more of these vastly many universes should be expected to have the right numbers for life. And of course it is only in such a universe that there would be observers, like ourselves, to wonder at our being here.

There are other and more exotic suggestions involving quantum theory, "chaotic inflation," and so on, that provide tenuous reasons for thinking that our empirical universe may be one of many. One or another of these many-universes explanations looks to be the most promising for straightforward scientific status.

Now the important point for our argument is that *if* all of these proposed explanations, especially the various many-worlds hypotheses, could be eliminated, the fine-tuning would then provide rather striking confirmation for the theistic hypothesis. But because we cannot definitively eliminate them, we need to consider the relative strength of the evidence supporting each.

I am in no position to give an up-to-date account of the status of these various quasi-scientific hypotheses. What can fairly be said of all of them, I believe, is that they are so highly speculative that none has much (if any) empirical confirmation apart from the role it plays in explaining the fine-tuning itself. A cosmologist friend pointed out that such work is supported in Britain by funds budgeted for mathematics rather than science. This shows, he said, how far this sort of work is removed from *empirical* science.

3.4 Further Confirmation

But what of the designer hypothesis? Has it additional confirmation apart from its value in explaining the fine-tuning? Yes. Here I need to use again the model (developed in chapter one) of the hierarchical relations among the sciences, including theology.

It is clear that each science in the hierarchy has its own proper sort of empirical data. The chemists have the results of spectrographic analyses. Biologists have microscopic views of cells. Psychologists have results of personality inventories. So the confidence we have in theories at each level is largely dependent on data appropriate to that level.

Another reason for confidence in any one theory is the way in which it is logically related to other theories at its own level. For example, the genetic theory lends immense support to the theory of evolution, and both these theories are at the level of biology.

Yet another kind of support comes from the links we can make from one level to its neighbors, both above and below, in the hierarchy. Suppose we have a theory at the biological level that a particular illness involves a hereditary predisposition that must be triggered by stress to manifest itself. This theory is confirmed when the gene responsible is actually located and mapped—it is then validated from below. It is confirmed from above when we do an epidemiological study and find that the illness generally appears after a major trauma, such as the death of a loved one or a divorce. This is confirmation from the psychological level.

Now how does all this apply to our designer hypothesis? First, remember that *our* design hypothesis is already tightly woven into a vast network of theory—we call these theories "theology." We claim not only to know that some intelligent being designed the cosmos, but also that this being is the God of Abraham and Sarah, the Father of Jesus Christ, our Lord and Redeemer.

In the previous chapter we looked at data available to confirm theological theories. I mentioned Christians' experiences in prayer and healing as evidence for the existence and power of the Holy Spirit. The divinity of Christ is confirmed both by historical events in the life of Jesus and by ongoing Christian experience testifying to his lordship.

There is one additional kind of support from below, from science, which gives the designer hypothesis a tremendous explanatory edge over other accounts of the fine-tuning. So far in this chapter I have been concentrating on the relations between theology and the natural-science side of the hierarchy. But there is a very significant phenomenon pertinent to the human-science side of the hierarchy that also cries out for explanation. It is simply this: the existence of religion. Most people in most societies in most historical eras have had some sort of religion. It is one of the most powerful forces in human life. What causes it? How are we to explain this phenomenon?

The reader may now be thinking, *That's simple; there is religion because there is God.* For believers, this explanation seems so obvious we often forget that, as with all hypotheses, other possibilities must be considered. Our own era, apparently, is unusual in the extent of its atheism and agnosticism. And in our era (the past century or two) a variety of competing nontheistic hypotheses have been invented to explain religion. There was Sigmund Freud's psychological hypothesis. This stated that believers are looking for the perfect father. There are a number of versions of the sociological hypothesis, which claim religions exist because they provide social cohesion.

So the situation is something like this: on the natural science side of the hierarchy we have a phenomenon, the fine-tuning, that cries out for explanation. There are a number of competing hypotheses, each of which might explain it. There is the chance hypothesis (Hc). There is the hypothesis of logical necessity (Hn). There are the various many-worlds hypotheses (Hm), and in addition there is the theological hypothesis (Ht).

The double arrows in the figure below are meant to indicate that the hypothesis is *supported* by the fine-tuning, insofar as it provides the best explanation of the fine-tuning (that is, to the extent the fine-tuning can be derived from the hypothesis deductively). So far, however, there is no way to choose the best explanation.

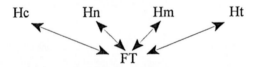

On the human-science side we have another and very different phenomenon that also cries out for explanation: religion. It too has a variety of possible explanations. Ht is again a theological hypothesis, Hp is the psychological hypothesis, and Hs is the sociological hypothesis. We can represent the situation as follows.

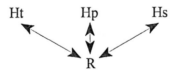

Now consider what happens when we combine these two figures:

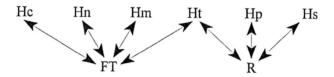

The point of this diagram is to show that the theological hypothesis has double support. Of course it is not that the theological theory has exactly twice as much support as the other hypotheses. The point is that independent confirmation of a theory, confirmation from an entirely different source, makes a great deal of difference in evaluating the theory. Unlike all of its competitors in cosmology, the designer hypothesis does have independent confirmation. So, from the point of view of philosophy of science, the design hypothesis at least for now is the best available explanation of the fine-tuning. This is the central claim that I have set out to defend in this chapter.[9]

4. The Place of Humans in the Cosmos

Before I conclude, I want to return to an issue I raised in chapter one. I claimed that evidence of other life in the universe raises afresh the question of where we, the human race, stand in the universe and in God's plans. The cosmological fine-tuning is relevant to this issue as well.

Consider again the verses from Psalm 8 with which I began this chapter.

> When I look at your heavens, the work of your fingers,
>> the moon and the stars that you have established;
> What are human beings that you are mindful of them,
>> mortals that you care for them? (Ps. 8:3-4)

How much more than the Psalmist are we able to appreciate the wonder of the cosmos itself! How much more can we, through these recent discoveries, appreciate that in a certain sense it all appears to have been created with beings like us in mind!

Since the Copernican revolution, humans have been removed from the center of the universe. We have discovered how small our planet is in comparison to the vastness of the universe. We have learned how short is our history in comparison to its age. Our view of the natural world has been "de-anthropocentrized."

But the present cosmological results show that if God were to have creatures such as ourselves, then the whole universe had to be created pretty much as it is in order for that to be possible. It had to have about as much matter in it—as many stars, galaxies, planets—and it had to be about as old as it is. We are not now at the center of the universe. However, it is certainly possible for believers to see ourselves as the point or end of it all. We can literally say that all the stars in the heavens, even the billions we cannot see, were in this sense created for our sake.

5. Summary

I began in chapter one by criticizing two common views of the relations between theology and science. There is the conflict model, expressing the views of the creationists: science and Christianity are competing for the same turf.

There is also what has been called the two-worlds model. This is the view commonly found among heirs of philosopher Immanuel Kant and theologian Friedrich Schleiermacher: science and religion are such different enterprises that they cannot possibly conflict or even affect one another. Often proponents of this view go on to emphasize the complementarity of science and faith. Science gives us the facts; religion gives us the "meanings" for human existence. Science gives us technology; religion gives us ethical guidance for its use.

In chapter two I criticized this science-religion dichotomy. Theology gives us genuine knowledge, not only about God but also about God's relations to human beings and to the entire cosmos. Therefore what theology has to say sometimes connects (positively or negatively) with what the sciences have to say. A complete view of reality must take both science and theology into account and strive for consistency if we find conflicts.[10] I proposed a third model for relating theology and science—a minority view but one now gaining in acceptance.

To illustrate this third model, I concentrated on an area where scientists themselves are groping for further explanation, and the question has been raised whether this fine-tuning is a case in which science itself can provide no answer. Even scientists with no prior religious motivations have suggested that the answer we need may be God.

So the Bible does not replace science (as it too often does for creationists) nor does it complement it in some other sphere or dimension. Rather the Bible complements (that is, completes) science in a straightforward sense. It tops off the hierarchy of the sciences. It answers the boundary questions that arise in science but go beyond science's competence to answer.

This means theology learns from science; for example, theology may have something to learn from the discovery of life on Mars. It also means that science can occasionally learn from theology. This, I am sure, is a much more startling claim. I hope to make good on it in the next chapters.

IV

Neuroscience and the Soul

1. A Potential Conflict?

What are humans made of? I know: bones, muscle, fat—everything one studies in biology class. But is that all? Most Christians, throughout most of our history, have believed there is another part, generally called the soul. This second part has been considered essential—it is often thought of as what is saved for eternal life or damnation. It is also thought to account for our capacity to be in relationship with God in this life.

Increasingly, though, our culture is developing an understanding of the human person that sees us as purely physical. Contributions to this newer view come from sciences such as biology but also from philosophical arguments. Most recently neuroscience, study of the brain and nervous system, has made it appear that the brain does most (or perhaps all) of the things people once attributed to the soul.

So it looks as if the Christian community may be headed for a conflict with science. My goal in this chapter is to point out that there is another option.

First we need to gain some historical perspective; the word *soul* has meant many different things at various points in church history. Then we'll turn to the neurosciences and consider the fascinating work going on there. Only after that will we turn to the difficult question of what the Bible has to say and what contemporary Christians should think about the issues.

2. Ancient and Medieval Views of the Soul

Many Christians are already aware that Christian philosophy has been influenced by Hellenistic or Greek patterns of thought. Although Christianity began among the Jews, it quickly spread throughout the Mediterranean world. Greek culture—Greek language, customs, ideas—had infiltrated all of those other Mediterranean cultures, much the way Western culture now influences much of the world. A crucial task for early theologians, apologists, and evangelists was to find ways of relating the gospel to those Hellenistic ways of thinking. This is much like what many missionaries do today. They go to a foreign country, study the ideas of the people there, and look for points of contact so the gospel will make sense to these people.

So it's important to know what ideas about the person were available in the Mediterranean world during the centuries when Christian theology was being developed. There was much confusion—just as there is today. *Today* there are materialists who say humans are nothing but atoms. *Then* there were the Epicurean philosophers, who said the body *and soul* are nothing but atoms. Today there are New Age thinkers who believe our bodies are animated by a little spark of the divine—in essence, our souls are part of God. Some held much the same view then.

We must not press the similarities too far; much has changed since the first centuries of the Christian era. For example, our knowledge of the nature of atoms has changed, so current materialists cannot be saying exactly the same thing as their predecessors. I simply want to make the point that early Christians also needed to address how best to relate the gospel to the culture's various theories of human nature.

Augustine (354-430) has probably been the most influential theologian since the Apostle Paul. For may centuries he nearly settled the question of the nature of the person. Philosophically educated, Augustine found a particular strand of philosophical thinking a useful tool for making Christian theology intelligible in his own day. This was Neoplatonism, so called because it was in Augustine's day a development of the ideas of the philosopher Plato, who had lived about 350 years before Christ.

Plato taught that the person is composed of two parts: a mortal body and an immortal soul. In fact, he believed the soul is eternal; it pre-exists the body and is only temporarily imprisoned in the body during earthly life. The soul's true home is a transcendental realm of "Ideas." The Neoplatonists developed a set of religious practices that involved suppressing the body and its drives to cultivate the soul and ensure its return to the transcendent realm at death.

Augustine's views are similar. Augustine taught that the person is composed of soul and body. The soul is immortal, not eternal, since it has a created beginning. He described the soul as using a mortal body—using rather than being imprisoned in it, since the doctrine of creation forbids considering the body evil.

How wonderful, some might think, that these pagan philosophers developed ideas so similar to Christian teaching! Careful. Plato's ideas may have been strangely *like* Christian ideas—or Christians may have simply borrowed some ideas *from* Plato.

Plato had a student, Aristotle, who developed strikingly different views on many subjects. During the first 1000 years of Western Christianity, Plato and his more loyal followers had been seen as the most useful resource for theologians, but during the Middle Ages Aristotle finally got his turn.

Thomas Aquinas (1225-1274) is famous for resolving conflicts between Christian theology (still largely dependent on Augustine) and the science and philosophy of Aristotle, introduced into European culture by the Arabs. Thomas continues to be influential among Catholic theologians. His interest for us now is that he developed a more sophisticated account of the soul than any of his predecessors (and perhaps anyone since). We need to consider all of these *functions* of the soul to see why contemporary neuroscience presents such a challenge.

We have to begin with the account of matter that both Thomas and Aristotle were using. For them, matter is passive. It has the potential to become all sorts of things, but only if some *active* principle affects it. The active part of any entity, on this view, is the *Form*. So every existing thing is composed of matter and form.

Living things have powers or capacities that go far beyond those of non-living things. Rocks, for instance, cannot grow or reproduce. This means living things must have more potent and interesting forms than do rocks. These more interesting forms are *souls*. Plants have economy-model souls—forms that give them capacities to take in nutrients, grow, and reproduce. These are nutritive or vegetative souls. Animals have nutritive powers but also the capacity to perceive things and move around. Our human souls give us all these capacities and more. We have the deluxe model—the *rational* soul.

Bear with me as I fill in the details of the faculties Thomas attributes to the human soul. The soul is thought of as having three major levels of functioning. I have already noted that the lowest powers of the human soul, shared with both plants and animals, are the vegetative faculties of nutrition, growth, and reproduction. Next higher are the sensory faculties, shared only with animals. These include the exterior senses of sight, hearing, smell, taste, and touch.

In addition, there are the four "interior senses." One is the *phantasia*, which simply means the imagination; another is the *vis memorativa*, the memory. We also share with the animals two other internal senses called the *vis aestimativa* and the *sensus communis*. The *sensus communis* is the faculty that distinguishes and collates the data from the exterior senses—for example, it accounts for our being able to associate the bark and the brownness and the feel of the fur with the same dog. The *vis aestimativa* allows for perceptions that go beyond sensory perception, such as recognizing that something is useful or friendly or unfriendly. Notice what a good cognitive psychologist Thomas was, to distinguish all these abilities involved in ordinary perceptions.

The sensitive or animal level of the soul also provides for the power of locomotion and for lower aspects of appetite—the ability to be attracted to sensible objects such as food or a mate. This appetitive faculty is further subdivided between a simple tendency toward or away from what is sensed as good or evil and a more complex inclination to meet bodily needs or threats with appropriate responses, such as attack, avoidance, or acquiescence. Together these appetitive faculties (all still at the sensory level) provide for eleven kinds of emotion: love, desire, delight, hate, aversion, sorrow, fear, daring, hope, despair, and anger.

The rational faculties are distinctively human. They include passive and active intellect and will. The two intellectual faculties together enable abstraction, grasping or comprehending concepts, judging, and remembering.

The will is a higher appetitive faculty whose object goes beyond things we can perceive with the senses. Remember, we share with animals the ability to be attracted to physical things such as food. So Thomas is saying we humans have an additional capacity to be attracted to good things of a different sort. In fact, he says, the object of this faculty is the good itself, which is God. Here is our commonsense notion that the soul is what enables us to relate to God. Morality is a function of attraction to the good combined with rational judgment as to what the good truly is. We will come back to this account of the soul shortly, as we consider some of the recent developments in neuroscience.

3. Developments in Neuroscience

3.1 The Story of Phineas Gage

First I turn to a story. My source is Antonio Damasio's fascinating book, *Descartes' Error*.[1] The story is of Phineas Gage, a twenty-five-year old construction foreman for the Rutland & Burlington Railroad. Gage is in charge of a group of men whose job is to lay tracks for the railroad's expansion across Vermont. This requires blasting the stone to make a straighter and more level path.

Gage is described as five-foot-six and athletic. In the eyes of his bosses, however, Gage is more than just another able body. They say he is "the most efficient and capable" man in their employ. This is good, because the blasting takes keen concentration. Several steps have to be followed: First, a hole must be drilled in the rock. After it is filled about halfway with explosive powder, a fuse must be inserted and the powder covered with sand. Then the sand must be "tamped in," or pounded with a careful sequence of strokes from an iron rod.

It is four-thirty on a hot afternoon in 1848. Gage has just put powder and fuse in a hole and told the man who is helping him to cover it with sand. Someone calls from behind. Gage looks away. Before his man has poured in the sand, Gage begins tamping the powder directly with the iron bar. The rod strikes a spark in the rock. The charge blows upward in his face.

> The [tamping] iron enters Gage's left cheek, pierces the base of the skull, traverses the front of his brain, and exits at high speed through the top of the head. . . . Phineas Gage has been thrown to the ground. He is stunned . . . silent but awake.

Gage was taken to a nearby hotel. The doctor who was called to tend him described the scene. "He at that time was sitting in a chair upon the piazza of Mr. Adams' hotel. . . . When I drove up, he said, 'Doctor, here is business enough for you.'"

Surviving the explosion with so large a wound to the head, being able to talk and walk and remain coherent immediately—this is all surprising, Damasio says. Gage's physical recovery was complete in less than two months. Gage could touch, hear, and see. He was not paralyzed of limb or tongue. He had lost vision in his left eye, but his vision was perfect in the right. He walked firmly, used his hands with dexterity, and had no noticeable difficulty with speech or language.

Yet this astonishing outcome pales in comparison with an extraordinary change in Gage's personality. "Gage's disposition, his likes and dislikes, his dreams and aspirations are all to change. Gage's body may be alive and well, but there is a new spirit animating it."

Gage's physician, Dr. Harlow, describes how the "equilibrium or balance, so to speak, between his intellectual faculty and animal propensities" had been destroyed. The changes became apparent as soon as the acute phase of brain injury subsided. He was now

> fitful, irreverent, indulging at times in the grossest profanity which was not previously his custom, manifesting but little deference for his fellows, impatient of restraint or advice when it conflicts with his desires, at times pertinaciously obstinate, yet capricious and vacillating, devising many plans of future operation, which are no sooner arranged than they are abandoned.

These new personality traits contrasted sharply with the "temperate habits" and "considerable energy of character" Phineas Gage possessed before the accident. He had had "a well balanced mind and was looked upon by those who knew him as a shrewd, small businessman, very energetic and persistent in executing all his plans of action." So radical was the change that friends and acquaintances hardly recognized the man. They noted sadly that "Gage was no longer Gage." So different a man was he that his employers had to let him go shortly after he returned to work. "The problem was not lack of physical ability or skill; it was his new character."

Damasio uses this story to introduce his research on brain localization. That is, by a careful analysis of Gage's skull, Damasio has been able to determine exactly which parts of the brain were destroyed by the iron rod. He infers from this and other similar cases that these specific regions are essential to the practical reasoning that Gage became incapable of performing.

3.2 Brain Localization Studies

Damasio's research is part of a growing body of data on regions of the brain responsible for various mental and emotional capacities. This research began with the study of patients incapacitated by tumors or strokes. Careful note was taken of their symptoms. After autopsy these symptoms could be correlated with the regions of brain damage. More recently, various sorts of brain scans have made it possible to study these correlations in living subjects.

These varied techniques have allowed for localization of a vast array of cognitive functions. For example, Broca's area in the left frontal region and Wernicke's area in the temporal lobe are involved in speech. Furthermore, more specifically located lesions can selectively affect the person's command of color vocabulary, common nouns, highly specific nouns, proper names.[2] There are also apparently social regions of the brain, such as those allowing for facial recognition and perception of emotion. Victims of localized damage may show "affective agnosia," the inability to recognize emotions.[3]

To summarize the impact of scientific developments in general and neuroscience in particular on contemporary conceptions of the person, I return to the human faculties Thomas attributed to the soul and mention scientific developments relevant to each.

First, the soul, for Thomas and other ancient and medieval thinkers, was the life principle. Today the most common criterion for death is "brain death," or cessation of all neural activity.

Recall that the functions of the nutritive or vegetative soul included growth, nutrition, and reproduction. These processes are fairly well understood now in biological terms, especially since the discovery of DNA. The brain is significantly involved here, too, in that neurochemicals play a large role in appetite and sex drive; pituitary hormones control growth.

The functions of the animal soul were locomotion and a variety of senses and appetites. Locomotion is now known to be controlled by the motor cortex, running across the top of the brain, and by the efferent nervous system (which is one half of the nervous system, running from the brain to the extremities; the other runs to the brain).

Great progress has been made in tracing the processes involved in sensation. For example, signals are transmitted from two different kinds of light-sensitive cells in the retina, through a series of processors, to the visual cortex. Smell involves signals from six different kinds of receptor cells in the nose transmitted to the olfactory lobes in the brain.

The task Thomas assigned to the interior sense of *sensus communis* is now studied by neuroscientists as "the binding problem." Remember, this is the task of associating input from the five senses to be able to perceive a single object.

Thomas' interior sense of memory has been much researched. Long-term memory is now envisioned as the result of patterns of connections in the neural network. Short-term memory is believed to be enabled by a system of "recurrent pathways." The idea is that information is processed, then recycled and fed into the process again. A part of the brain called the hippocampus is involved in converting short-term into long-term memory, but how this happens is not yet known.

I have already mentioned the localization of specific sorts of memory. Paul Churchland has drawn a map of the brain showing regions involved in language memory. Different locations are responsible for verb access, proper name access, common noun access, and color terms.[4] The parietal lobes are involved in memory of faces.

PET scans make it possible to record localized elevations of neuronal activity. Churchland reports an experiment in which his wife Patricia was asked to perform a task involving her visual *imagination*. (Remember that one of Thomas' four interior senses was *phantasia* or imagination.) The activity in her visual cortex was elevated exactly during the time she was doing the exercise in imagination, but not as much as when she was gazing at the external world. Churchland hypothesizes that visual imagination involves the systematic stimulation of the visual cortex "by way of *recurrent* axonal pathways descending from elsewhere in the brain."[5]

Thomas' *vis aestimativa* included ability to distinguish between the friendly and the unfriendly, the useful and the useless. One clear instance of this is our ability to read others' emotions. While there does not seem to be a single location responsible for this capacity, there are patients whose brain damage has resulted in its loss. A patient called "Boswell" suffers from extensive lesions to the frontal pole of both temporal lobes and to the underpart of the frontal cortex. One among many of his mental deficits is the inability to perceive emotion. Churchland reports:

> I watched as Boswell was shown a series of dramatic posters advertising sundry Hollywood movies. He was asked to say what was going on in each. One of them showed a man and a woman, in close portrait, confronting one another angrily. The man's mouth was open in a plainly hostile shout. Boswell, without evident discomfort or dismay, explained that the man appeared to be *singing* to the woman.[6]

Thomas' sensitive appetite was responsible for such emotions as desire, delight, sorrow, despair. Studies of causes of mental illnesses involving troubling emotions, such as depression, have shown a significant role for neurotransmitters such as serotonin. Neurotransmitters are chemicals involved in conveying signals from one neuron to another.

The higher mental faculties that Thomas attributed to the rational soul are less understood. However, all involve language. Thus even if we do not understand *how* they depend on brain functioning, we know *that* they do because of the close association of linguistic abilities with specific brain areas, especially Wernicke's and Broca's areas.

The appetitive function attributed to the rational soul was, for Thomas, the ground of moral behavior. Here we return to Phineas Gage. His intellectual capacities were undamaged, but the part of his brain needed to desire the higher things of life was destroyed. In Thomas' language, he lost the appetite for the good, which is to say he lost his appetite for God.

The foregoing is a brief sketch of points at which biology and neuroscience have provided accounts of the dependence on physical processes of *specific* faculties once attributed to the soul. It is interesting to note in addition the rough analogy between Thomas' (and Aristotle's) three levels in the soul's hierarchy of faculties (nutritive, animal, and rational) and the gross anatomy of the human brain. We share with the lower animals the reptilian complex at the base of our brains, which is responsible for territoriality, sex drive, and aggression. With the higher animals we share the limbic system, responsible for emotion. We alone have a large and highly developed neo-cortex, responsible for theoretical reasoning.

So the reptilian complex and limbic system together provide for many of the functions attributed to the two lower levels of the soul. The function of the neo-cortex corresponds quite closely with those attributed specifically to the rational soul.

What does all this mean? It is important to remember that the specific concepts of the soul Western Christians have used were developed by philosophers to account for capacities that seemed not attributable to the body alone. It appears that Plato and Aristotle and Thomas may simply have been wrong.

4. Biblical Accounts of the Person

Some readers may be objecting that theological accounts of the soul did not originate with Plato and Aristotle but with the Bible. The Old Testament is full of references to the soul. It was written largely before Plato and certainly independently of any philosophical developments in ancient Greece.

True, but the issue is not so simple. Here are a few familiar lines from the Psalms (KJV).

> "For thou wilt not leave my soul in Hell" (16:10).
> "O keep my soul, and deliver me; let me not be ashamed. . ." (25:20).
> "Gather not my soul with sinners" (26:9).
> "[They that trust in their wealth] like sheep they are laid in the grave; death shall feed on them . . . but God will redeem my soul from the power of the grave: for he shall receive me" (49:14-15).

Such passages fit nicely with a view that, while the body may decay in the grave, God saves souls. This sounds like body-soul dualism. However, there are other references to the soul in the Psalms that do not fit this dualist picture.

> "O Lord my God in thee do I put my trust: save me from all them that persecute me. . . . Lest he tear my soul like a lion, rending it in pieces" (7:1-2).
> "Deliver my soul from the sword" (22:20).
> ". . . without cause have they hid for me their net in a pit, which without cause they have digged for my soul" (35:7).

There is something amiss. Souls are not capable of being torn or stabbed. And it is bodies that people throw in pits. Even stranger—

> "And if any of the flesh of the sacrifice of his peace offering be eaten at all on the third day, it shall not be accepted. . . it shall be an abomination, and the soul that eateth of it shall bear his iniquity" (Lev. 7:18).

Souls eating meat? What's going on here?

It is widely agreed now that the Hebrew word translated "soul" in all these cases—*nephesh*—didn't really mean what we post-Augustinian Christians have meant by soul. In most of these cases, soul is simply a way of referring to the whole living person. Here's how the New International Version translates some of these same passages (emphasis added).

KJV: "For thou wilt not leave my soul in hell";
NIV: "because you will not abandon *me* to the grave" (Ps. 16:10).
KJV: "O keep my soul, and deliver me; let me not be ashamed;"
NIV: "Guard my *life* and rescue me; let me not be put to shame" (Ps. 25:20).
KJV: "the soul that eateth of it shall bear his iniquity";
NIV: "the *person* who eats of it will be held responsible" (Lev. 7:18).

So the Hebrew word *nephesh* is translated as "person," "life," or just used as a way for a person to refer to him- or herself. It's also used of animals; here it is best translated as "living being." Those who have seen body-soul dualism in the Old Testament, including many of the earlier translators, have been reading it into the texts rather than getting it out of them.

The next question is this: What does the New Testament teach about body-soul dualism versus physicalism? This is a more difficult question, but I believe the best answer is—nothing! Let me explain.

There are a number of issues on which the Bible has clear *teachings*. There are other things the Bible *says* to put forward those teachings. For example, when Isaiah says God will gather Israel and Judah from the four corners of the earth (Isa. 11:12), he doesn't mean to teach that the earth has four corners. That's a conception of geography and geology he simply assumed in making his prophecy.

I believe the new Testament has much to teach about what it means to be human. However, it does not mean to teach specific details about how many parts we're made of, whether body and soul; body, soul, and spirit; or just one.

Just as in our own day, there were in New Testament times a variety of ideas about the makeup of the person. The various New Testament authors used different ideas to make clear their teachings on other matters. So if we try to go through the New Testament to see what it teaches on this subject, we'll end up frustrated and confused.

Does that mean Christians can believe anything they want about the makeup of persons? Not at all. Some views are compatible with Christian teaching, some not. Let me list four current theories, then suggest that two extreme views are ruled out for Christians but two in the middle are consistent with Christian teaching.

The first view, already explored, is Plato's understanding that humans are composed of two parts, an eternal soul that is trapped in a perishable body. The person is identified with the soul. The goal of life is to escape from the body. As already mentioned, this view is inconsistent with Christian theology because it implies that the body (and the rest of the material world) is evil. This contradicts our doctrine of creation: God created the material world and saw that "it was good." It also runs counter to our understanding of incarnation. The son of God took flesh—not just as a temporary disguise, but forever. Christian hope lies not in a soul escaping, but in the promise that we shall be raised, bodily, just as Jesus was. So this radical Platonic dualism is out of bounds for Christians, as Augustine recognized 1500 years ago.

At the opposite end of the spectrum of views is reductive materialism. This is the view that humans are nothing but physical bodies. And—here is a significant addition—everything about us can be explained in purely naturalistic terms. That is, science can explain our moral behavior as being programmed by our genes. Religious experience can be explained as abnormal neurological events, similar to hallucinations. The very existence of religion can be explained sociologically—we create religion to foster social cohesion. So human beings are a part of the natural world, and there is nothing more to be said about us. We are just intelligent animals, who fool ourselves when we think we have moral obligations or a relationship with God. This account of human nature is radically opposed to Christian teaching, but it is one common in secular academic circles.

So these are the extreme positions. Plato said we were eternal souls; some contemporary thinkers say we're nothing but biological organisms. In between are two other possibilities, which we may call holistic dualism and nonreductive physicalism. I want to suggest that both are consistent with Christian teaching—or at least are equally consistent, since there are minor problems with each.

Holistic dualism is the view that we are indeed composed of two parts. We can use the terms *body* and *soul*, but both parts are essential. We are only truly ourselves when the two parts are united and functioning harmoniously together. Thus it may be possible for the two aspects of the person to come apart temporarily at death, but we are not really ourselves again until the body is restored at the resurrection.

This holistic dualism has been the most common position in church history, at least from Augustine to the present century. It would be difficult to argue on theological grounds that it is wrong. It is not possible here to asses how well such dualism fits with all New Testament language. But developments in science certainly call this view into question. Notice that developments in neuroscience can never *prove* there is no soul; one can always look at the localization studies and say functions of the soul are just surprisingly well-correlated with certain brain functions. But the concept of the soul seems more and more an unnecessary complication.

So it is worthwhile to ask about the fourth possibility, nonreductive physicalism. This is a view that on the surface may seem the same as the reductive materialism I criticized earlier, in that there is only one entity, the person, who is clearly a physical, biological organism. However, I argue that what neuroscience shows is that such an organism is indeed capable of all of those higher human capacities that have been attributed to the soul. It is our brain and neurological system that gives us the capacities to think about right and wrong and sometimes to choose to the good. Our brain, with its large neo-cortex, is what enables us to recognize God's holiness, to recognize a still small voice as the word of God.

I believe nonreductive physicalism is close to the ancient Hebrew conception of the person. It maintains the *holistic* view of the person found in both the Old and New Testaments. It has theological advantages over dualism. Most important, it forces us to attend to New Testament teaching about bodily resurrection as the source of Christian hope for eternal life.

Notice that I use the same term here, nonreductive physicalism, that I used in chapter one to refer to my account of the relations among the sciences. This view of the person fits nicely into that hierarchical account of reality. As we go up the hierarchy of the sciences, we first study subatomic particles. These combine to form atoms. Atoms bond together to form molecules—and here we are at the level of chemistry. Large, complex molecules make up the substance of living beings: proteins and DNA, for instance. Here we are at the level of biology.

Remember that ancient philosophers believed that to get living things, a non-material soul had to be added to matter. Into the nineteenth and even twentieth centuries, many biologists believed something needed to be added to non-living matter to get life—a vital force or "entelechy." That view has now been rejected. What is needed is not a different kind of part, a non-material one—but a special organization of the parts.

My argument in this chapter is that when we get to the level of psychology we do not need to add another non-material part, such as a mind or human soul, to get a human being. Consciousness and all of our other human traits depend instead on a special organization of the brain. So a nonreductive physicalist account of the person fits nicely into this model of the sciences.

What I said in chapter one about top-down causation is crucial. Humans can act in a top-down manner in lower levels of the hierarchy, just as God can act in a top-down manner influencing us. So it is important not to confuse this model with a reductionist account, in which only bottom-up causation is recognized.

5. The Anabaptists and "Soul Sleep"

I noted above that there are problems with both nonreductive physicalism and holistic dualism. Here I want to consider one problem with nonreductive physicalism—the teaching concerning an intermediate state between death and the general resurrection.

I mentioned that Augustine adopted a dualist account of the person, according to which humans possess an immortal soul. The question then was how to reconcile this Greek-influenced account of life after death with the Christian teaching on resurrection of the body. The solution was to say that at death the soul is separated from the body. Resurrection amounts to God's provision of a new and glorified body at a later time.

It followed naturally from Aristotle's conception of the soul that it simply ceases to exist when the body dies. Thomas, however, went to great lengths to argue that the human soul survives death and thus has a degree of conscious experience during the time between death and resurrection.

In light of controversies over purgatory and the expectation of the imminent return of Christ, this issue of the intermediate state became prominent during the Reformation. Many reformers, especially within the radical wing, argued that the soul "sleeps" preceding the resurrection and Last Judgment. Since *sleep* is a euphemism in the New Testament for death, there are actually two possibilities here—that the soul actually dies with the body or that it is, in some sense, asleep. Some, such as the Polish Anabaptist Simon Budny, taught the more radical view. Here the understanding is that the soul is but the life of the body and so ceases to exist at death. More commonly, the radicals taught that the soul continues to exist yet in an unconscious state.

John Calvin attacked both sorts of views, beginning with a treatise called *Psychopannychia* (1545). This word actually means a watchful or sentient "wake" of the soul but nonetheless has come to be associated instead with the two positions Calvin was opposing.[7] Calvin's teaching on the conscious intermediate state has settled this issue for many of his followers. The same teaching had been made official for Catholicism by the Fifth Lateran council in 1513.

So it appears a nonreductive physicalist account of the person presents problems for Christians of both the Catholic and Reformed traditions. If there is no soul, and the nervous system is the seat of consciousness, then how can there be a wakeful state between death and resurrection?

Such a problem does not arise for Christians in the Radical Reformation tradition. While most of the early leaders of these movements did assume a form of body-soul dualism, there was no move to harden such an assumption into doctrine. Mennonite or Brethren theologians today have no intermediate state with which to come to terms. Although it is comforting to think of our deceased loved ones as already enjoying the presence of God, it is more consistent with the physicalist view to accept the conclusion that we all await resurrection at the end of history.

6. Summary

I began by suggesting that Christians may be headed for a major conflict with science. This is because Christians tend to hold to a dualistic view of the person as body and soul, whereas science seems to suggest that we are all of a piece. However, if you ask contemporary Christians what exactly the soul is, they will probably say it is the part of us that relates to God and survives death but will not have a clear idea beyond that.

For this reason I took time to look at what major Christian theologians had to say on the matter, especially Thomas Aquinas. He provided an impressive list of our human capacities and even figured out which part of the soul was responsible for each. Then I turned to the neurosciences to show how many of these capacities are now understood as functions of the brain and nervous system.

Next I pointed out that we have been mistaken to think that the Old Testament offers a dualist account of the person. Instead, we have been misled by the way later Christians translated the Hebrew texts. That forced us to ask what the New Testament has to say. I claimed that the New Testament writers are actually relatively silent about this issue. However, there are topics about which the Bible teaches that definitely rule out certain views, such as the sort of body-denying dualism that Plato invented and the reductionistic materialism that some scientists and philosophers promote today.

I suggested that this leaves us with two theologically acceptable views of the person. Each could be supported by proof-texts from the New Testament, but the real question is whether the views are compatible with the rest of Christian theology. Both nonreductive physicalism and holistic dualism seem to be usable accounts, although there are minor problems reconciling each with the theological tradition.

The main doctrinal problem with nonreductive physicalism, in the eyes of many Christians, is the doctrine of the intermediate state. However, I suggested that this should be much less of a problem for Christians in the Radical Reformation tradition than for Catholics or for Christians in the Reformed tradition.

So I am not urging rejection of dualism by those who hold it. What I hope to have accomplished here is to show that Christians have some options. If in the future developments in science and philosophy make it clear dualism no longer makes sense, that need not threaten Christian faith. We may even find that nonreductive physicalism fits better than dualism with much of the Bible. It may be one of those cases in which a development in science helps us see more clearly than we could before what is in our scriptural texts.

V

Christianity and Evolution

1. Overview

Not since the days of Copernicus and Galileo has a scientific issue so preoccupied Christians as the theory of evolution. Charles Darwin published *The Origin of Species* in 1859. Nearly 150 years later Christians are still divided over what to make of it.

I mentioned in chapter one the preference of media people for stories about conflict. As a result, it is easy to overlook the fact that many Christians have no objections to evolutionary theory. So while I focus here on sources of conflict between Christianity and evolutionary theory, I want to emphasize that many have found it not only possible but helpful to their Christian understanding to conceive of biological life in evolutionary terms.[1]

The first purpose of this chapter is to survey reasons some Christians oppose evolutionary biology. However, my main focus will be what Radical Reformation Christians ought to think about these issues. I will try to show, on the one hand, that many of the issues that concern sisters and brothers in other traditions are not Radical Reformation issues. On the other hand, there are uses made of evolutionary biology to which Anabaptists have special reason to object.

2. Historical Reasons for Objections to Evolution

In chapter three I described William Paley's brilliant argument for the existence of God based on the fitness of organisms to their environments and the apparent design of their organs to serve specific purposes. Appreciation of the popularity of this argument among Christians in Darwin's day is helpful for understanding why evolutionary theory was such a bombshell. Darwin argued that a combination of random variation and natural selection was sufficient to account both for the development of effective organs and appendages and for the remarkable adaptation of organisms to their environments. We can learn a lesson from this bit of history: never to put all our apologetic eggs in one basket![2]

A second source of controversy has had to do with human conceptions of our place in the universe. In short, many Christians have been insulted by the claim that we are closely related to the animals. However, I believe this reaction is unjustified, particularly for people of the Bible. The creation stories in Genesis indeed make the point that humans have a special role in the created order and in relation to God—we are made "in the image of God." Yet they testify equally to our continuity with the rest of nature—we are made "of the dust of the earth." The play on words in Hebrew—*'adam* is made of *'adamah,* earth*—can be captured in English: we are *humans* made from *humus*.

So I suspect Christian objections to kinship with animals come not from the Bible but from Greek philosophy, wherein all of reality was conceived of in terms of a hierarchy of value. Humankind was thought to occupy a distinct rung on this metaphysical ladder, above the animals but just below divine beings.

This issue is closely related to the topic of chapter four: through their souls humans shared kinship with divinity. Consequently, a strategy used to reconcile theology and biological evolution has been to maintain that though the human *body* may have evolved from animal life, the human *soul* is a special creation by God. Pope John Paul II affirmed this view in an address to the Pontifical Academy of Sciences on October 22, 1996. Similar attitudes have appeared in recent discussions of cloning. Some commentators have asserted that cloning of humans should be strictly prohibited because, while one might clone bodies, one could not thereby clone a human soul.

Christians in Darwin's day also objected to evolutionary theory because of its association with ethical and social applications now referred to as "social Darwinism." The argument here is that competition for survival results in evolutionary progress in the biological realm. Therefore this competition should be allowed and even encouraged in the human world as well, and no provision should be made to encourage the survival and propagation of the weaker members of society. However, it is not clear whether Darwinian theory was the source of such theories or whether Darwin's concept of the survival of the fittest was influenced by the economic and social theories already in existence in his day in Britain.[3] Some current biologists argue that the emphasis on struggle and competition is a one-sided account. It needs to be balanced with appreciation for cooperation among organisms, both within species and across species. We shall return to these issues below.

Finally, much of the resistance to evolutionary biology can be traced to limited views of divine action. The problem is to suppose that an event must be *either* an act of God *or* a natural event. To my knowledge, Christian theologians have always denied such a strict opposition. For instance, medieval theologians described God as the primary cause of all events and natural causes as secondary or instrumental.

In the early modern period, however, the concept of a law of nature developed. This was originally a theological notion (a metaphor) to express God's governance of the natural world. Just as God governs humans by means of law, so too God governs the motions of the planets by law. Gradually, however, the metaphorical and theological nuances were lost. God was still seen by many to be the source of the laws of nature, but the laws were granted a force and status of their own.

The question then arose whether God acted in any other way than by creating both the universe and the laws of nature at the beginning. Isaac Newton believed that God in addition had to intervene occasionally to adjust the orbits of the planets. Later still, Pierre Simone de Laplace became famous for denying the need for any such intervention.

So Christians had become used to the idea that one could distinguish between acts of God and the regular processes of the natural world (the world of physics and astronomy). Darwin's achievement can be described as bringing the phenomena of life under the rule of natural laws.[4]

Given this pattern of thinking about divine action, the claim that the origin of life could be explained in terms of natural laws has seemed to some a *denial* of divine action. But what is needed here is to recall longstanding Christian teaching that God is an agent in every event, not only as creator, but also as sustainer and governor of all that exists.

A common strategy for reconciling evolutionary theory with Christian theology has been to claim that God has created living things by working *through* the evolutionary process. Recall the description of the hierarchy of the sciences I developed in chapter one. Using this model we can see that the same event can be described at a number of levels. For example, we can describe a long and complex molecule in chemical terms as DNA, or we can describe it in biological terms as the gene for green eyes.

The benefit of recognizing theology as one of the levels in his hierarchy of description is to make it clear that a theological account and a biological account can both be true and valuable descriptions of the same set of processes. The biologist looks for the natural antecedents of a biological event and seeks patterns among these chains of events. The theologian can describe the same series of events in terms of God's purposes and achievements.

3. Current Objections to Evolution

Perhaps it is surprising that I did not mention conflict with Genesis as a major reason for rejection of Darwin's theories. There was, of course, some of this. But it needs to be emphasized that the issue as often understood today, in terms of *literal* reading of an *inerrant* text, has only become central in our own century. In particular, this means reading the first chapters of Genesis as though they are historical or scientific accounts of the origin of the universe and of life.

Some current literalists would like us to believe theirs is the original reading strategy, but this is not the case. Christians from earliest days have recognized that there are various kinds of literature in the Bible. Each kind deserves to be read accordingly. The notions of literal reading and inerrancy arose around the beginning of this century as a reaction against historical-critical study of the Bible and as part of the modernist- fundamentalist controversy within mainline Protestantism.

The problem described above concerning divine action seems to be as much an issue now as it was in Darwin's day. Some Christians suppose that if science can explain the origin of life, this automatically conflicts with the claim that life was created by God. I claimed in chapter three that divine action is one of the most significant theological issues of our day. In fact, I believe it lies behind much of the disagreement among contemporary Christians about how to read Scripture.

The question of divine action is thus more fundamental than the controversy over biblical literalism. That is, if divine acts and natural events are thought to be mutually exclusive, then the process of revelation is likely to be understood as a direct intervention into human history, and it will not be possible to give adequate attention to the human character of the biblical texts. However, if God's action is understood ordinarily to take place in and through natural and historical processes, then one can recognize both the human and divine authorship of Scripture. A natural consequence will be a reading strategy that takes into account the contexts and purposes of the human authors.

Another reason for negative assessments of evolutionary theory by Christians is also related to the issue of divine action. Some scientists and philosophers, as well as some Christians, assume that if scientific explanations can be given of natural processes, then this rules out theological accounts. As a result, biologists such as Will Provine and Richard Dawkins, cosmologists such as Carl Sagan, and philosophers such as Daniel Dennett promote evolutionary biology as evidence that religious claims are false. Some develop what might be called "naturalistic religions."

Carl Sagan is probably the best known of these due to his popular video series, *Cosmos*. Sagan begins with plain old biology and cosmology but then uses concepts drawn from science to fill in what are essentially religious categories. These categories fall into a pattern surprisingly parallel to the Christian conceptual scheme. Sagan has a concept of ultimate reality: "the Universe is all that is or ever was or ever will be." He has an account of ultimate origins: Evolution with a capital "E." He has an account of the origin of sin: the primitive reptilian structure in the brain, which is responsible for territoriality, sex drive, and aggression. His account of salvation is gnostic in character—that is, it assumes that salvation comes from knowledge. This knowledge is scientific and perhaps advanced by contact with extra-terrestrial life forms more advanced than we.[5]

The model of the hierarchy of the sciences is helpful in understanding this phenomenon. I argued in chapter one that the sciences raise boundary questions they alone are not competent to answer. Thus for an intellectually satisfying account of reality, one needs some account of ultimate reality at the top of the hierarchy. Christians, of course, can turn to theology. But without some recognizable theological system at the top of the hierarchy, there is an "empty space" that cries out to be filled. Sagan and others oblige by creating new scientistic religions.

Biology in particular raises boundary question concerning the meaning of human life. The evolutionary process is subject to chance in a number of ways. It is easy to imagine replaying cosmological and evolutionary history and getting a very different set of animal species. There is no guarantee, from what biology can tell us, that *Homo sapiens* would evolve again. Are we not then just a remarkable cosmic accident?

Atheistic worldviews do need to be addressed by Christians, but I argue that the goal should not be to discredit evolutionary theory but to show where legitimate claims of evolutionary biology end. That is, the science itself needs to be distinguished from the religious and metaphysical speculations that these "evangelical atheists" add to it. Further, more needs to be done to incorporate interpretations of this and other scientific theories into our Christian worldviews.

4. What is at Stake for Radical Reformation Christians?
4.1 How to Read Scripture

The controversy over biblical literalism is not—or should not be—a focus for Christians in the Radical Reformation tradition. John Howard Yoder points out that in the Anabaptist communities the interpretation of Scripture took place within the context of the need for guidance in questions concerning the congregation's practice. He writes,

> Thus the most complete framework in which to affirm the authority of Scripture is the context of its being read and applied by a believing people that uses its guidance to respond to concrete issues in their witness and obedience. Our attention should center not on what theoretical ideas a theologian (isolated from the church) can dissect out of the text of Scripture in order to relate them to one another in a system of thought. As the apostle Paul says, it is for teaching, reproof, correction, and instruction in right behavior.[6]

This practical approach to Scripture is in sharp contrast to one that treats the texts as a book of facts, scientific or otherwise. It invites us to ask, what were the immediate needs of the people of God for whom the creation stories were first written or told? One point on which many scholars agree is that the first creation story (Gen. 1–2:4a) was written in response to Babylonian creation myths. Its purpose is theological rather than scientific or historical. No brief summary can do justice to this beautiful piece of literature, but we can at least say that its teachings include testimony to the absolute power of God and the goodness of creation. This is in contrast to pagan epics that depict creation as the result of a struggle between the gods and forces of chaos.

New Testament scholar Walter Wink emphasizes that pagan creation myths stand behind the acceptance of war and injustice as a normal part of human life. The *Enuma Elish* dates from around 1250 BCE but is based on much older traditions. Here the universe is said to have been created out of the body of a murdered goddess. The gods themselves set the pattern of domination and warfare. The implication is that the very substance of which humans are created is tinged with violence. Furthermore, warfare and domination are necessary to prevent the cosmos from reverting to the chaos from which it was created.[7]

So here is the tale that gives meaning to mainline Western culture. It was repeated in Greek and Roman mythology. It continues today in nearly all of the literature and television programming used to socialize children: it is the story of the good guy preserving order by means of violence. It lies behind much of modern social-scientific research, which I shall argue in the next chapter assumes that violence is necessary to maintain social order. Unfortunately it has had all too deep an influence on mainstream Christianity, showing up thinly disguised in the just war tradition from Augustine to the present.

So the practical import of the biblical account of origins is not to forestall scientific descriptions of how the universe or the human race came to be. Rather, it is to assure us that the possibility for goodness, justice, and peace is built right into the universe, from the very beginning.

4.2 Evolutionary Ethics

The practical focus of Radical Reformation Christianity means that ethical issues associated with evolutionary biology ought to be of great concern to us. I questioned above whether historically (a) evolutionary theory led to social Darwinism; or (b) arguments for rapacious capitalism inspired Darwin's picture of nature. Whatever the historical sequence, it is certainly the case that biology now poses serious challenges for Christian ethics.

One challenge is sociobiology. Sociobiologists claim to provide a naturalistic account of human morality. They explain altruism, for instance, as the product of natural selection. That is, some suggest that because altruistic actions are most often beneficial for family members, who share many of the same genes, altruism therefore increases the chance of survival *for one's genes*. The development of the trait is thereby explained by natural selection.[8]

What strikes me about this argument is how un-Christian is the ethic it is taken to explain. Or, to put it the other way around, if this is the "ethic" of the biological world, then Christian morality is profoundly anti-biological. We Christians are not enjoined to sacrifice most for those who are biologically closest to us. Quite the contrary! Jesus' teachings are shockingly anti-family. Instead, the Christian's first loyalty must be the new family of God, which is one new "race," made out of both Jews and Gentiles. Now, of course, this race includes all races. If anyone is to be singled out for special care it is the "other"—the stranger, the enemy.

The second challenge to Christian morality (and this is a special challenge to churches that teach nonviolence) is this: If God is creator of the whole world, then we ought to look for signs of God's character and of God's will for our lives in the natural world, as well as in Scripture. It is often said that there are two books in which God is revealed—the Bible and the Book of Nature.

But biologists now call our attention to the "moral" character of the evolutionary process. How many times have we heard of "nature red in tooth and claw"? How can we reconcile an ethic of self sacrifice—even unto death—with this picture of nature as a scene of competition and survival of the fittest? If we Christians are to imitate the character of God, what are we to make of a God who has chosen to create through such a bloody process?

The issue of human distinctiveness is relevant here, as well as our discussion in the previous chapter of the nature of the person. I pointed out that ancient Greeks conceived of humans as occupying a middle position in a hierarchy, with spiritual beings above and animals below. Our immortal soul was our "ticket" to the realm of the divine. Ethics could be conceived as wisdom about how to further distance ourselves from the "beastly" beasts.

But the proper hierarchy for Bible readers needs no such series of gradations. There are two basic metaphysical categories for us: God and creation—God and not-God. It is clear where we belong in this scheme.

Holmes Rolston emphasizes our continuity with the rest of the biological world and at the same time reconciles evolutionary morals with a Christian ethic of self-sacrifice. In both cases, in the life we are called to live as followers of Jesus and in the biological realm, there is an analogy with the self-sacrificing character of God. In brief, Rolston teaches us to see the work of God not in the predator but in the prey. I quote his beautiful prose at length.

> The Earth is a divine creation and scene of providence. The whole natural history is somehow contained in God, God's doing, and that includes even suffering, which, if it is difficult to say simply that it is immediately from God, is not ultimately outside of God's plan and redemptive control. God absorbs suffering and transforms it into goodness.

Rolston describes nature itself as "cruciform." The universe is not a paradise but a theater where labor and suffering drive us to make sense of things. "Life is advanced not only by thought and action, but by suffering, not only by logic but by pathos."

This pathetic element in nature is seen in faith to be at the deepest logical level the pathos in God. God is not in a simple way the Benevolent Architect, but is rather the Suffering Redeemer. The whole of the earthen metabolism needs to be understood as having this character. The God met in physics as the divine wellspring from which matter-energy bubbles up . . . is in biology the suffering and resurrecting power that redeems life out of chaos.

So Rolston suggests that, in faith, the secret of life is seen to lie not in natural selection and the survival of the fittest; rather "the secret of life is that it is a passion play. Things perish in tragedy. The religions knew that full well, before biology arose to reconfirm it."

[T]hings perish with a passing over in which the sacrificed individual also flows in the river of life. Each of the suffering creatures is delivered over as an innocent sacrificed to preserve a line, a blood sacrifice perishing that others may live. We have a kind of "slaughter of the innocents," a nonmoral, naturalistic harbinger of the slaughter of the innocents at the birth of the Christ, all perhaps vignettes hinting of the innocent lamb slain from the foundation of the world. They share the labor of the divinity. In their lives, beautiful, tragic, and perpetually incomplete, they speak for God; they prophesy as they participate in the divine pathos. All have "borne our griefs and carried our sorrows."

The abundant life that Jesus exemplifies and offers to his disciples is a life of sacrifice, "a sacrificial suffering through to something higher. There is something divine," he says, "about the power to suffer through to something higher."

The cruciform creation is, in the end, deiform, godly, just because of this element of struggle, not in spite of it. There is a great divine "yes" hidden behind and within every "no" of crushing nature. God, who is the lure toward rationality and sentience in the upcurrents of the biological pyramid, is also the compassionate lure in, with, and under all purchasing of life at the cost of sacrifice.

While God rescues from suffering, Christian faith never teaches that God eschews suffering in the achievement of the divine purposes. Seen in the paradigm of the cross, God too suffers, not less than creatures, in order to gain for them a fuller life.[9]

This interpretation of suffering is consistent with Anabaptist thought, in which the suffering of Christians is not generally seen as a punishment for sins, but rather as redemptive participation with Christ in the expected consequences of obedience to God in the midst of a sinful world. Hans Hut proclaimed "the Gospel of Christ crucified, how He suffered for our sake and was obedient to the Father even unto death. In the same way we should walk after Christ, suffering for his sake all that is laid upon us, even unto death."[10]

It is interesting to note that several of the original Anabaptist writers extended this account of human suffering to include "the Gospel of All Creatures." Hut himself taught that the suffering of animals and the destruction of other living things conforms to the pattern of redemption through suffering, and in its own way preaches the gospel of Christ Crucified.[11] The parallels with the writings of Holmes Rolston are striking.

4.3 A Coherent Worldview

John Howard Yoder claims that the ministry of Jesus has not only social-ethical and historical significance, but *cosmic* significance.

> Then to follow Jesus does not mean renouncing effectiveness. . . . It means that in Jesus we have a clue to which kinds of causation, which kinds of community-building, which kinds of conflict management, go with the grain of the cosmos, of which we know, as Caesar does not, that Jesus is both the Word (the inner logic of things) and the Lord ("sitting at the right hand"). It is not that we begin with a mechanistic universe and then look for cracks and chinks where a little creative freedom might sneak in (for which we would then give God credit): it is that we confess the deterministic world to be enclosed within, smaller than, the sovereignty of the God of the Resurrection and Ascension. . . .

"[C]ross and resurrection" designates not only a few days' events in first-century Jerusalem but also the shape of the cosmos.[12]

Yoder points out that cosmological language of the first century would have referred to the sociopolitical world in its metaphysical-religious setting, rather than to the natural world. Yet we cannot help asking what difference it makes to our view of the *physical* cosmos if the affirmation of John's Prologue is true, if this Jesus is the Word through whom all things came to be.[13] Is there any sense in which this conception of God, revealed in the cross and resurrection of Jesus, finds confirmation in contemporary natural science?

I intend to argue in the next chapter that an ethic of self-sacrifice and nonviolence, drawn from our Radical Reformation theology, can be made consistent with the social sciences. This can be done only with difficulty, however, since these sciences incorporate judgments about possibilities for human sociality at odds with ours. In this section I wish to indicate a few ways in which the natural sciences can contribute to a unified account of God, human life, and the rest of creation.

In contrast to an account that sees the material cosmos as the ultimate reality and our own existence as merely a surprising accident, we tell the story of a God who, in the words of James Wm. McClendon,

> is the very Ground of Adventure, the Weaver of society's Web, the Holy Source of nature in its concreteness—the one and only God, who, when time began, began to be God for a world that in its orderly constitution [cosmological fine-tuning] finally came by his will and choice to include also—ourselves. We human beings, having our natural frame and basis [in the evolutionary process], with our own (it seemed our own) penchant for community, and (it seemed) our own hankerings after adventure, found ourselves, before long, in trouble. Our very adventurousness led us astray; our drive to cohesion fostered monstrous imperial alternatives to the adventure and sociality of the Way God had intended, while our continuity with nature became an excuse to despise ourselves and whatever was the cause of us. We sin. In his loving concern, God set among us, by every means infinite wisdom could propose, the foundations of a new human society; in his patience he sent messengers to recall the people of his Way to their way; in the first bright glimmers of opportunity he sent—himself, incognito, without splendor and fanfare, the Maker amid the things made, the fundamental Web as if a single fiber, the Ground of Adventure risking everything in this

adventure. His purpose—sheer love; his means—pure faith; his promise— unquenchable hope. In that love he lived a life of love; by that faith he died a faithful death; from that death he rose to fructify hope for the people of his Way, newly gathered, newly equipped. The rest of the story is still his—yet it can also be ours, yours.

That is the fundamental love story of Christian faith, or rather a brief allusion to that story whose telling in full must exhaust all skill and consume all words (see John 21:25). To outsiders the story is sure to count as a myth among myths, but to us it is no myth, but our only way of telling the whole truth.[14]

McClendon emphasizes that faithful, costly, and redemptive suffering in Christian love is a necessary ingredient in the continuation of this story of God and God's community. I have followed Rolston and Hans Hut in extending this recognition to the natural world as well. In an analogous way, all sentient beings participate in the suffering that comes from the fact that what God created is not God, it is other than God. Only through God's slow travail does that which is closer to God emerge from that which is totally other.

In light of this story, we can look at the fine-tuning of the cosmological constants as God's provision, from the very beginning, for a universe with sufficient time and complexity to allow a species to evolve that has the capacity to "image" God. This capacity includes not only sensing (in a dim and faltering way) the subtlety of the design of the cosmos itself, but also, by following the example of Jesus, imitating the moral character of God.

This image is not dependent on a nonmaterial soul inserted into the physical cosmos at some point in the creative process. Rather, the image emerges from the increased complexity of our physical being, which allows for intelligence, freedom, and social relatedness. The image of God appears when we imitate the life of Jesus, who did not count Godly prerogatives something to be grasped, but humbled himself, becoming a servant of all (cf. Phil. 2:6-8).

Thus in our social relations we are called to imitate the God who sacrificed the power to be the sole determinant of history to make room for our independence. This self-sacrifice is costly, sometimes deadly, but we have the assurance that God's plans for creation do not end with the world as we know it. They will be fulfilled in a transformation prefigured in the resurrection of Jesus.

5. Summary

A brief parable by John Wisdom has become something of a classic in philosophy of religion.

> Two people return to their long neglected garden and find among the weeds a few of the old plants surprisingly vigorous. One says to the other, "It must be that a gardener has been coming and doing something about these plants." Upon inquiry they find that no neighbor has ever seen anyone at work in their garden. The first man says to the other, "He must have worked while people slept." The other says, "No, someone would have heard him and besides, anybody who cared about the plants would have kept down these weeds." The first man says, "Look at the way these are arranged. There is purpose and a feeling for beauty here. I believe that someone comes, someone invisible to mortal eyes. I believe that the more carefully we look the more we shall find confirmation of this." They examine the garden ever so carefully and sometimes they come on new things suggesting that a gardener comes and sometimes they come on new things suggesting the contrary and even that a malicious person has been at work. . . .[15]

Through this story I want to sum up the point of this chapter. In the parable we can distinguish two levels of description, and a third is implied. The two characters could describe what they see in purely botanical terms—for instance, "The roses are vigorous, but the iris bed is choked with weeds."

There is a higher level of description, which I shall call the aesthetic level, based on but not determined by the botanical facts, such as "The arrangement of the plants shows a feeling for beauty."

Finally, there is what I shall call the intentional-level description: "Some gardener must tend these plants."

Similarly, in describing the natural world, there are a variety of levels of description, from physics through cosmology, from biology through the social sciences. I shall argue in the next chapter that some account of ethics, based on insight about the *purpose* of it all, provides a link to theology—or at least to *some* account of Ultimate Reality. Our concern in this chapter is evolutionary biology.

Here it is important to distinguish three levels of description. At the bottom is evolutionary biology itself—a story about the gradual emergence of more complex biological forms. This account provides a basis for but does not determine a moral-level description. I emphasized that two very different accounts of the moral nature of the biological world can be used to interpret the facts of evolution. The social-Darwinist account emphasizes competition for survival—nature red in tooth and claw—and pronounces it good. I have emphasized that we need not identify with the predator, but rather with the prey, and see prefigured there the Lamb of God.

Each of these moral accounts is dependent on a yet higher level of description, an account of Ultimate Reality. For the materialist the cosmic process itself is ultimate. For us, there is a longer story, beginning before the Big Bang and continuing beyond the various "ends" that physical cosmologists can project—a story whose loveliness must in its telling "exhaust all skill and consume all words."

VI

Radical Reformation Theology
and Social Science

When he saw the crowds he went up a mountain. There he sat down,
and when his disciples had gathered round him he began to address
them. And this is the teaching he gave:
Blessed are the poor in spirit; the kingdom of Heaven is theirs.
Blessed are the sorrowful; they shall find consolation.
Blessed are the gentle; they shall have the earth for their possession.
Blessed are those who hunger and thirst to see right prevail; they
shall be satisfied.
Blessed are those who show mercy; mercy shall be shown to them.
Blessed are those whose hearts are pure; they shall see God.
Blessed are the peacemakers; they shall be called God's children.
Blessed are those who are persecuted in the cause of right; the
kingdom of Heaven is theirs.
Blessed are you, when you suffer insults and persecution and
calumnies of every kind for my sake. Exult and be glad, for you have
a high reward in heaven; in the same way they persecuted the
prophets before you.
—Matthew 5:1-12 (REB)

1. Radical Christianity

I am a convert to the kind of Christianity that descends from the
Anabaptist or Radical Reformation heritage. The moment I knew I had
to make the change came in reading the life of Michael Sattler.[1] Sattler
had been a Catholic, as I was at the time. Later he became one of the
most significant leaders of the little group of Swiss Brethren who began
the Radical Reformation. We know of him primarily because of two
things: his role in a conference held on the Swiss-German border in the
town of Schleitheim, and his death.

The Schleitheim confession presented the Anabaptist distinctives,
those points on which the radicals differed from the other Protestants.
These were the seven distinctives:

1. baptism was to be reserved for believers;

2. unrepentant sinners were to be admonished and, if necessary, banned from the congregation;

3. the breaking of bread was to be reserved for those baptized and at peace with one another;

4. the church was to be separated from the world;

5. shepherds (pastors) were to be chosen from among the congregation;

6. "concerning the sword," that Christians should not use any punishments other than the ban to enforce church discipline and should not engage in combat or any other civic duties that involve violence;

7. Christians should not swear loyalty oaths to the government.

Soon after the meeting at Schleitheim, Sattler was imprisoned, charged with heresy, and executed.

> When the judges returned to the room the verdict was read, as follows: "In the matter of the prosecutor of the imperial majesty versus Michael Sattler, it has been found that Michael Sattler should be given into the hands of the hangman, who shall lead him to the square and cut off his tongue, then chain him to a wagon, there tear his body twice with red hot tongs, and again when he is brought before the gate, five more times." When this is done to be burned to powder as a heretic. . . .
>
> Whereafter on May 20 [1527] he was led to the marketplace and the judgment which had been pronounced was executed against him. After cutting off his tongue he was chained to the cart and according to the verdict torn with red hot tongs; then burnt in fire. Nevertheless, at first in the square and then again at the place of execution he prayed to God for his persecutors and also encouraged others to pray for them and finally spoke thus: "Almighty eternal God, Thou who art the way and the truth, since I have not been taught otherwise by anyone, so by Thy help I will testify this day to the truth and seal it with my blood."[2]

Jesus said, blessed are the peacemakers, they shall be called God's children; blessed are those who are persecuted in the cause of right, the kingdom of Heaven is theirs; blessed are you when you suffer insults and persecutions of every kind for my sake. It was so clear to me, when I read of Sattler's execution and of the many others carried out by Protestants and Catholics alike in the name of God, that Jesus must be on the side of those dying, not those doing the killing and torturing. It was clear what side I would have had to be on, had I been I alive in those frightening days.

That is why I left the church in which I had grown up and which I had loved so deeply. After wandering through a variety of "believers churches," I now find myself in the Church of the Brethren. This Anabaptist community emerged in Germany nearly two centuries after the original Radical Reformation but was founded on the same teachings as the Mennonite churches.

A number of the Anabaptist distinctives are now commonplace. Many churches practice believers baptism; their pastors are there by congregational agreement rather than being appointed by the state. *All* churches agree that the sword, hot tongs, or drownings are not to be used to compel people to be "good Christians." However, Anabaptists remain at odds with many Christian churches regarding whether we are duty-bound to take up the sword to defend our countries.

2. Conflict and Consonance between Theology and the Sciences

So far in this book I have presented a relatively non-conflictual account of the relations between science and Christianity. I have not endorsed the creationists' view that modern biology must be defeated if Christianity is to flourish. In fact, I suggested in chapter three that if we accept the evolutionary account of the origins of life, then investigate the conditions necessary for a universe in which that process can take place, we find ourselves with some fascinating evidence for God's creation of the universe. God is the Master Tuner who planned the cosmological constants in such a way that the universe would be, in Isaiah's words, not a formless waste, but a place to be lived in.

So there is a positive relation between Christian theology and the *natural* sciences. Christian doctrine answers the boundary questions that arise at the edge of scientific cosmology: why is there a universe at all, and why, among all the billions and billions of possibilities, is it a universe suitable for us to live in? Because this hypothesis of God's creative activity is the most parsimonious explanation, not only of the fine-tuning but of a number of other facts as well, it is confirmed by the scientific evidence.

However, remember that in chapter one I did not claim that science and Christianity *cannot* conflict. If we deny the two-worlds view, and claim that it is possible for religion and science to interact, then it is possible for them to conflict. I believe there are a number of striking conflicts between Christianity and the *social* sciences. The place to look in Scripture to locate the conflicts is not the creation stories in Genesis, but the Sermon on the Mount.

3. Ethics in the Hierarchy of the Sciences

To make good on this claim, I need to introduce another discipline into my model of the hierarchy of the sciences, namely, ethics. I place it between theology and the social sciences. This gives us the following picture:

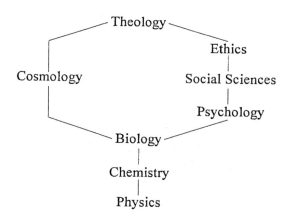

I argue below that the social sciences make a number of assumptions about what is good for human life in terms of social and political order, civil justice, and so forth. They also make a number of assumptions about what kinds of good it is *possible* for humans to achieve.

Now, the question of what are the ultimate goods for human societies to pursue is an ethical question. The social sciences cannot decide this for themselves. The social sciences need the discipline of ethics to answer questions they can raise but not answer satisfactorily. Here we have another boundary question—one that arises at one level of the hierarchy but calls for an answer from a higher level.

In addition, I shall argue that theology should have a top-down influence on both ethics and the social sciences. The teaching of Jesus, especially as Mennonites, Brethren, and Quakers have understood it, provides a radically different view of the possibilities for human good. In light of this teaching, ethical assumptions within the social sciences must be questioned.

Before I proceed, let me acknowledge that the view I shall present here, of the mutual relations among theology, ethics, and the social sciences, is philosophical heresy. Two dogmas of the modern intellectual world have been the so-called fact-value distinction, and the exclusion of God from the intellectual world—that is, the thesis that the existence of God makes no difference to intellectual pursuits.

The fact-value distinction is enshrined in the slogan that "You cannot derive an ought from an is." What is at issue here is the relation between judgments belonging to the realm of ethics or morality and statements about the way the world is. The modern doctrine has been that there are two distinct spheres. And the moral sphere is autonomous—not logically dependent on any other.

Immanuel Kant, the great Enlightenment philosopher, helped formalize this dichotomy between science and ethics. He distinguished not only two subject matters, but also two reasoning faculties—pure reason and practical reason. Kant's motivation for this distinction was in part to protect human freedom. That is, to insulate the human will from the determinism of Newtonian science, he believed it was necessary to distinguish the sphere of "noumena," including the self, from the phenomenal world, governed by the laws of physics. Then he argued that it is absolutely illegitimate to argue from science to ethics.

So the fact that ethics, the systematic study of morality, was *not* to be placed in the positivists' hierarchy of sciences represented a victory for Kant. However, there was a negative side to this development. Whereas Kant believed ethics had a solid rational foundation of its own, which would serve as a basis for adjudicating ethical disputes, it has not turned out to be so. Its logical connections to an all-encompassing worldview sundered, ethics has grown more and more fragmented. One result is the appalling moral relativism we find in our society.

4. The Exclusion of God from Academia

An equally important characteristic of late modern thought has been the exclusion of God from academia. I do not mean, of course, that there are no religion courses, or that many academics are not believers. My point is that what one believes about God is supposed to be a private matter that makes no difference to one's views in either the natural or the social sciences.

As philosopher Bruno Latour puts it, "No one is truly modern who does not agree to keep God from interfering with Natural Law as well as with the laws of the Republic." This "crossed-out God" is distanced from both Nature and Society, yet kept presentable and usable nonetheless." Spirituality was reinvented," he says, creating a situation in which

> the all-powerful God could descend into men's heart of hearts without intervening in any way in their external affairs. A wholly individual and wholly spiritual religion made it possible to criticize both the ascendancy of science and that of society, without needing to bring God into either. The moderns could now be both secular and pious at the same time.[3]

In effect, the late modern world offers the scholar three sealed compartments: the sciences, the moral sphere, and the religious sphere. My claim, in sharp opposition to these two modern dogmas, is that these three need to be related to one another. The social sciences raise questions that only ethics can answer, but the discipline of ethics itself needs theology. Without God's revelation in Jesus, we have no way of knowing what is the ultimate purpose of human life, or what are the highest goods human beings can reasonably strive to attain.

Let us look more closely, then, at the relations between the social sciences, ethics, and theology.

5. Social Science, Ethics, and Theology

It has often been argued that the social sciences can be and must be "value-free." That is, they only describe social reality as it is, or at most provide information for making limited means-ends calculations. For example, if you wish to avoid shortages and surpluses, then you should institute a free-market economy. However, it is becoming increasingly common to recognize that there are ethical positions already incorporated into the social sciences.

5.1 The Assumption of the Necessity of Violence
For an example of the role of ethical assumptions in social theory, consider modern positions on the necessity for violent coercion in society. This assumption can be traced to the early modern philosophy of Thomas Hobbes. Hobbes claimed that the state of nature, prior to the social contract, is the war of each against all. The sovereign must have the right to impose the death penalty in order to maintain social order.

A variety of social theorists since then have claimed that coercion is necessary to maintain society, and that violence is merely the ultimate form of coercion. For example, sociologist Max Weber's classic statement on the relation between politics and violence is found in his essay "Politics as Vocation."

> Ultimately, one can define the modern state sociologically only in terms of the specific *means* peculiar to it, as to every political association, namely, the use of physical force . . . the state is a relation of men dominating men, a relation supported by means of legitimate . . . violence.[4]

Theologian and ethicist Reinhold Niebuhr has influenced a generation of policymakers with the thesis he developed in *Moral Man and Immoral Society*. The needs of an institution for its very survival require the people involved in it to do things they would not do (and would not be morally justified in doing) as individuals. Niebuhr's thesis has been dubbed with the congratulatory title of "Christian realism." In the Preface to *Moral Man*, he says,

> The thesis to be elaborated in these pages is that a sharp distinction must be drawn between the moral and social behavior of individuals and of social groups, national, racial, and economic; and that this distinction justifies and necessitates political policies which a purely individualistic ethic must always find embarrassing. . . . In every human group there is less reason to guide and check impulse, less capacity for self-transcendence, less ability to comprehend the needs of

others and therefore more unrestrained egoism than the individuals, who compose the group, reveal in their personal relationships. . . . When collective power, whether in the form of imperialism or class domination, exploits weakness, it can never be dislodged unless power is raised against it.[5]

More recently, sociologist Peter Berger has concurred that there is inevitably an element of coercion required for society not to be destroyed by the disruptive forces within it. "Violence," he says, "is the ultimate foundation of any political order."[6]

Now, I set out to provide an example of an ethical assumption found within the social sciences, but in what sense is this an ethical assumption? Is it not, rather, simply a statement of empirical fact, a law of human behavior? The very fact that one theorist I have quoted—Niebuhr—is known primarily as a Christian ethicist might at least make us suspicious that we are not dealing with pure social fact.

Niebuhr's views on the possibility of non-coercive, nonviolent social structures depended on a prior ethical judgment regarding the highest good for humankind. This view of the human good is in turn the consequence of a particular theological doctrine. Niebuhr wrote,

> Justice rather than unselfishness [is society's] highest moral ideal. . . . [T]his realistic social ethic needs to be contrasted with the ethics of religious idealism. . . . Society must strive for justice even if it is forced to use means, such as self-assertion, resistance, coercion and perhaps resentment, which cannot gain the moral sanction of the most sensitive moral spirit. . . .[7]

Niebuhr's judgment that justice is the highest good that can reasonably be expected in human history is in turn based on his eschatology—that is, on his theological views regarding the end of time. He believes that salvation, the kingdom of God, the eschaton, are essentially *beyond* history. Why does he hold this view of eschatology? He sets up the problem in terms of the relation between the finite and the infinite, the temporal and the eternal. Since it is not possible to conceive of the eternal being realized in the temporal, he concludes that the kingdom of God is *beyond* history. This in turn means that guilt and moral ambiguity must be permanent features of the interim.

Weber's justification is also overtly ethical: it is based on a distinction between an "ethic of ultimate ends" and an "ethic of responsibility." The ethic of ultimate ends is concerned with pure intent and pure means. The ethic of responsibility is concerned with the politically foreseeable results of one's actions in a political order where imperfection and evil are presupposed. The political realist is committed to achieving his ends even at the expense of morally dubious means. And, as already noted, the decisive means for politics is violence.[8]

So this is one example of the way ethical theories—theories about the ultimate good for humankind—are woven right into social-scientific reasoning. That is, we have here a social-scientific *justification* of the use of violence, based on the claim that a society simply cannot survive without it. But how do we know a society must resort to violence? This claim is based not on empirical facts, but rather on views about what is possible in history, before the eschaton. The claim is based on theology—but someone else's, not Mennonite or Brethren theology.

The contrasting Anabaptist views about what is possible in history can be justified by turning once again to Jesus' words in the Sermon on the Mount. Blessed are the poor in spirit, the gentle, those who hunger and thirst to see right prevail, those who show mercy, the peacemakers, those persecuted in the cause of right (Matt. 5:1-12). This passage begins and ends with "the kingdom of Heaven *is* theirs." This is present tense, not future tense. The kingdom of Heaven is already realized in history, right now, among those who adopt the peaceful, gentle way of Jesus.[9]

5.2 The Church as Social Experiment

Why did the radicals emphasize the separation of the church from the world? Because it is the church's job not merely to theorize about alternative social structures, but to provide empirical evidence that an alternate society is possible. A society based on reconciliation, a society that uses no violence, a society whose ultimate form of punishment is nothing harsher than the request to leave the fellowship—such a society can actually exist. By showing this possibility, Christians are light to the world.

In Matthew's Gospel, Jesus goes on to teach about reconciliation.

> You have heard that they were told, "An eye for an eye, a tooth for a tooth." But what I tell you is this: Do not resist those who wrong you. If anyone slaps you on the right cheek, turn and offer him the other also. . . .
>
> You have heard that they were told, "Love your neighbor and hate your enemy." But what I tell you is this: Love your enemies and pray for your persecutors; only so can you be children of your heavenly Father, who causes the sun to rise on good and bad alike, and sends the rain on the innocent and the wicked. If you love only those who love you, what reward can you expect? Even the tax-collectors do as much as that. If you greet only your brothers, what is there extraordinary about that? Even the heathen do as much. There must be no limit to your goodness, as your heavenly Father's goodness knows no bounds (Matt. 5:38-39; 43-48 REB).

Here, in brief, is the theological justification for the ethic that Jesus teaches. Why are disciples required to accept injury without repaying it? Because that is the very nature of God.

So here is a theological position, an account of the character of God, which justifies, in a "top-down" manner, an ethical stance, a particular way of living. I have emphasized the aspects of Christian ethics that are most distinctive among Anabaptists, but of course the whole of Jesus' moral teaching is included as well.

It is not unusual to claim that Christian ethical positions follow from Christian theology. However, I am making a further claim. I am claiming that from Christian ethics, understood from a Radical Reformation perspective, there follows a different vision of what is possible and normative in human social life. This vision is sharply at odds with the vision that has become normative in the social sciences. They claim that state-sponsored violence is necessary for the preservation of society. Anabaptists believe violence can be eliminated from human relations—violence is the exception, not the norm, of social life.

5.3 A New Vision for Social Science

If basic assumptions underlying sociology and political science and jurisprudence were called into question, what sort of social sciences might emerge? There would be a great deal for social scientists to do. Here is a concrete example.

The penal justice systems in many countries, including the U. S. and Canada, operate on the principle of *retribution*. The sentences given are understood largely as punishment, even though there is some talk of rehabilitation. But Jesus' teaching suggests an entirely different theory of criminal justice. In the passage just quoted from Matthew's Gospel, Jesus repudiates the retributive system of an eye for an eye, a tooth for a tooth.

His teaching stimulates us to envision alternatives. In fact, there have been and still are alternatives. Throughout much of history, crime has been understood as an offense of one person against another, and people have assumed that the central response must somehow be to make things right again. Pre-Norman Celtic societies as well as many Polynesian, African, Asian, and Caribbean societies had *restorative* justice systems. The community or state had a role in promoting restitution, but the transaction was primarily between the victim and the offender.

A major change took place in English law at the time of William the Conqueror, when the state came to be seen as the ultimate victim of all crime. This was the beginning of a punitive system aimed not at restitution to the victim but at upholding the authority of the state.

Now we live in societies where the criminal justice system has taken over "responsibility" for vengeance on behalf of its citizens. But this means the victims have also lost their responsibility *and opportunity* to forgive.

Jim Consedine, a prison chaplain in New Zealand, describes a variety of non-retributive, restorative justice systems. One is an experiment in New Zealand involving reinstitution of the Maori justice system in children's court.

In this system, the role of the court is to bring together the offender and the victim, as well as the families or support groups of both parties. The judge and other officials of the state are present to facilitate a process that includes an opportunity for the victim to describe in personal terms the suffering and loss that has been occasioned. The families of both victim and offender also speak of their grief. The offender is given a chance to express regret, which happens in approximately ninety percent of cases. In such cases, the victims often forgive the offender. The penalties agreed upon by the participants are aimed only at making restitution to the victims, not at harming the offender. Consedine says,

> sometimes moving gestures of healing come from the victim side. They waive their right to compensation from an unemployed young offender who cannot afford it. They invite them to their home for dinner a week after the conference. They help to find an unemployed young offender a job, a homeless young person a home. In one amazing case, a female victim who had been robbed by a young offender at the point of a gun had the offender live in her home as part of the agreed plan of action.[10]

Now many would say that such a system could not work in our society. Yet Consedine has amassed quite a lot of evidence of the inefficiency of the retributive system and a respectable amount of evidence that restorative systems work. Consedine presents evidence showing a *negative correlation* between tougher sentencing and reform. Here are a few of the numbers he reports.

> In the period 1985-92 incidents of violent crime [in New Zealand] rose by 41 percent, despite a nearly two-thirds increase in the length of prison terms for such offenses. Statistics in New Zealand also revealed a three percent decrease in overall crime figures in the year ended 30 June 1994. Many areas of criminal offending—traffic, fraud, burglaries, thefts—showed a marked drop in offending rates. The two areas where offending rose substantially against this national trend, violent crime and drug offending, were the two areas where penalties had increased most in the previous 10 years. The rationale behind increasing the penalties at the time was one of deterrence.[11]

The United States imprisons at a rate of 520 per 100,000, four times that of New Zealand, which has the second highest rate; five times that of Britain; sixteen times that of Ireland. Yet a young American man is twenty times more likely to be murdered than an Englishman or a Dane.[12] So despite the political popularity of the notion that more and harder prison time makes the streets safer, there seems to be a great deal of evidence against this assumption.

For the success of the re-instituted Maori system in children's court in New Zealand, the results are as follows: Only 10 percent of youthful offenders go through the regular court system, down from 30 percent. Of the cases handled through the restorative system, 90 percent reach agreements. The rate of youth offenses has dropped from 64 per 1000 to 16 per 1000. The number of prosecutions of defendants aged 17-19 has dropped by 27 percent between 1987 and 1992.[13]

The point I wish to make by referring to Consedine's research is this: If more social scientists were gripped by a picture of the nonviolent, self-sacrificial social relations that Jesus describes, and less in the thrall of Reinhold Niebuhr's and others' "realism," there would be a great deal of research dedicated to cases such as this—studies of practical means by which that New Testament vision can be approximated in real life. The result might be not only a more optimistic picture of human sociality, but one that has the further advantage of being true.[14]

6. Summary

It is time to sum up. A variety of thinkers in a variety of disciplines are calling for review of modern assumptions. One set of such assumptions has been the disconnection of the social sciences from the natural sciences, the disconnection of ethics from science, and the exclusion of God from all spheres of intellectual discourse.

In this chapter I have developed a model for thinking about the relations among theology, ethics, and the sciences that understands them as hierarchically ordered and intrinsically interconnected. There are aspects of reality at each level of complexity that can be explained reductively, in terms of lower levels. But there are also boundary questions, requiring explanation from higher levels of discourse. Cosmology and physics raise boundary questions that can appropriately be answered theologically. The social sciences raise questions that can only be answered by turning to ethical systems. Ethical systems in turn raise theological questions.

Now, some who read an argument such as this are likely to suppose that this questioning process—which ends in both cases with theology—means that all knowledge is ultimately grounded in theological claims. All is based on faith. Some might approve that conclusion. Others will object that it is relativistic, since there are countless theologies available. Consequently it has been necessary to comment on scientific reasoning.

I claimed in chapter two that theology is very much like a science, in that it proceeds by means of hypothetico-deductive reasoning. One begins with a phenomenon to be explained. One asks what hypothesis, if true, would explain it. Then one tests the various hypotheses proposed by drawing further consequences from each and seeing how they square with the facts.[15] I claimed that theology has its own proper sorts of data, and that theological theories, such as the doctrine of creation, can find additional support when we show their explanatory value at lower levels in the scientific hierarchy.

All of this is meant to show that theology has a significant role to play in the academy as well as in the church. I made the bold claim that theology has as much to contribute to science as it has to learn from science. In particular, I argued that the social sciences could learn a great deal from the vision of sociality taught by Jesus and modeled, if only imperfectly, by believers' churches.

Notes

Chapter One: Relating Theology and the Sciences

1. Ian Barbour, *Issues in Science and Religion* (New York: Harper and Row, 1966); *Religion for a Scientific Age* (New York: Harper and Row, 1990).

2. Immanuel Kant, *Religion within the Limits of Reason Alone* (1793).

3. Friedrich Schleiermacher, *The Christian Faith*, ed. H.R. Mackintosh and J.S. Stewart (Edinburgh: T. & T. Clark, 1928).

4. David C. Lindberg and Ronald L. Numbers, eds., *God and Nature: Historical Essays on the Encounter between Christianity and Science* (Berkeley: University of California Press, 1986), 1.

5. Lindberg and Numbers.

6. Margaret Wertheim, "Does the Bible Allow for Martians?" *The New York Times* (August 11, 1996).

7. Quoted by Wertheim.

8. See George Lindbeck, *The Nature of Doctrine* (Philadelphia: Westminster, 1984), 94.

9. This rough model is well accepted in general outline, but it does not give a complete account of the sciences and the relations among them. For example, it provides no place for the historical sciences, and some sciences, such as genetics, cut across several levels.

10. It is actually more accurate to say that the positivists, Otto Neurath, in particular, aimed to reduce all of the sciences, including physics, to a more basic level dealing only with reports of sensory experiences. See P.M.S. Hacker, *Wittgenstein's Place in Twentieth-Century Analytic Philosophy* (Oxford: Blackwell, 1996), 59.

11. This latter term has the advantage both of being recognized in contemporary philosophy of mind and also, for Christians, of avoiding the atheistic connotations of "naturalism" and "materialism."

12. See *Critical Realism: A Study of the Nature and Conditions of Knowledge* (New York: Russell and Russell, 1966); first published 1916.

13. *The Philosophy of Physical Realism* (New York: Russell and Russell, 1966), 5; first published 1932.

14. Roy Wood Sellars, *Principles of Emergent Realism: The Philosophical Essays of Roy Wood Sellars,* W. Preston Warren, ed. (St. Louis, Mo.: Warren H. Green, Inc., 1970), 136-38.

15. *The Philosophy of Physical Realism*, 4.

16. See Donald T. Campbell, "'Downward Causation' in Hierarchically Organised Biological Systems," in F.J. Ayala and T. Dobzhansky, eds., *Studies in the Philosophy of Biology: Reduction and Related Problems* (London: Macmillan, 1974), 179-86; quotation 180. For a summary of the literature on top-down causation, see Arthur Peacocke, *Theology for a Scientific Age*, 2nd ed., (Minneapolis: Fortress Press, 1993), chap. 3.

17. I first suggested the branching model in "Evidence of Design in the Fine-Tuning of the Universe," in Robert Russell, Nancey Murphy, and C.J. Isham, eds., *Quantum Cosmology and the Laws of Nature: Scientific Perspectives on Divine Action* (Vatican City State and Berkeley: Vatican Observatory and Center for Theology and the Natural Sciences, 1993; distributed by University of Notre Dame Press), 407-35. For further refinements see Nancey Murphy and George F.R. Ellis, *On the Moral Nature of the Universe: Theology, Cosmology, and Ethics* (Minneapolis: Fortress Press, 1996).

18. See Arthur Peacocke, *Creation and the World of Science* (Oxford: Clarendon Press, 1979); and *Theology for a Scientific Age*, 2nd ed. (Minneapolis: Fortress Press, 1993).

Chapter Two: Theology as a Science

1. For my most detailed examination of this issue, see Nancey Murphy, *Theology in the Age of Scientific Reasoning* (Ithaca, N.Y.: Cornell University Press, 1990).

2. E.Y. Mullins, *The Axioms of Religion: A New Interpretation of the Baptist Faith* (Philadelphia: American Baptist Publication Society, 1908), 173-74.

3. Charles Hodge, *Systematic Theology*, 3 vols. (New York: Scribner's Sons, 1891), 1:9-15. First published 1871.

4. The suggestion is Carl Hempel's. Although the form of reasoning we are discussing here has been recognized for a long time, it was Hempel who gave it the name "hypothetico-deductive." See his elegant exposition in *Philosophy of Natural Science* (Englewood Cliffs, N.J.: Prentice-Hall, 1966).

5. Described by Hempel in *Philosophy of Natural Science*, 3-6.

6. I find Wolfhart Pannenberg's arguments for the historicity of the resurrection quite compelling. He rightly criticizes biblical scholars and theologians who use the principle of analogy in a wooden way to rule out as historical any acts of God. Instead, he argues that the same form of reasoning as used in science, hypothetico-deductive, should be used in this case. Then the resurrection can be shown to be the most plausible hypothesis to explain what we find in the texts. See *Jesus—God and Man*, tr. Lewis L. Wilkins and Duane A. Priebe (Philadelphia: Westminster Press, 1968).

7. However, the sayings I have used here are among those widely claimed to be authentic.

8. Jonathan Edwards, *A Treatise Concerning Religious Affections*, in John E. Smith, ed., *The Works of Jonathan Edwards*, vol. 2 (New Haven: Yale University Press, 1959); and Edwards, *The Distinguishing Marks of a Work of the Spirit of God*, in C.C. Goen, ed., *The Works of Jonathan Edwards*, vol. 4 (New Haven: Yale University Press, 1972).

9. Thomas Kuhn, *The Structure of Scientific Revolutions*, 2nd ed. (Chicago: University of Chicago Press, 1970).

Chapter Three: Cosmological Fine-Tuning and Design

1. See my *Beyond Liberalism and Fundamentalism: How Modern and Postmodern Theology Set the Theological Agenda* (Valley Forge, Pa.: Trinity Press International, 1996), chap. 3.

2. For proceedings of the first three conferences, see Robert J. Russell, Nancey Murphy, and C.J. Isham, eds., *Quantum Cosmology and the Laws of Nature: Scientific Perspectives on Divine Action* (Vatican City State and Berkeley, Calif.: Vatican Observatory and Center for Theology and the Natural Sciences, 1993); Robert J. Russell, Nancey Murphy, and A.R. Peacocke, eds., *Chaos and Complexity: Scientific Perspectives on Divine Action* (Vatican City State and Berkeley: Vatican Observatory and Center for Theology and the Natural Sciences, 1995); and Robert J. Russell, William R. Stoeger, and Francisco J. Ayala, eds., *Evolutionary Biology: Scientific Perspectives on Divine Action* (Vatican City State and Berkeley, Calif.: Vatican Observatory and Center for Theology and the Natural Sciences, 1998).

3. Two prominent books are John D. Barrow and Frank J. Tipler, *The Anthropic Cosmological Principle* (Oxford: Oxford University Press, 1986); and John Leslie, *Universes* (London and New York: Routledge, 1989). The figures above are from Leslie.

4. In William Paley, *Natural Theology; or, Evidences of the Existence and Attributes of the Deity, Collected from the Appearances of Nature* (1802).

5. Quoted by Elmer Sprague, in "William Paley," *Encyclopedia of Philosophy*, Paul Edwards, ed. (New York: Macmillan, 1967), 6:20.

6. David Hume, *Dialogues concerning Natural Religion* (1779).

7. For a more detailed account and evaluation, see George F.R. Ellis, "The Theology of the Anthropic Principle," in Russell et al. eds., *Quantum Cosmology and the Laws of Nature*, 367-405; for a more popular presentation, see Ellis, *Before the Beginning: Cosmology Explained* (London and New York: Boyars/Bowerdean, 1993).

8. See Barrow and Tipler, *The Anthropic Cosmological Principle*.

9. For a more detailed argument, see my "Evidence of Design in the Fine-Tuning of the Universe," in Russell et al., eds., *Quantum Cosmology and the Laws of Nature*, 407-435.

10. For a sample of (very different) positions that fall into this category, see Arthur R. Peacocke, *Theology for a Scientific Age*, 2nd ed. (Minneapolis: Fortress Press, 1993); and Nicholas Wolterstorff, *Reason within the Bounds of Religion*, 2nd ed. (Grand Rapids, Mich.: Eerdmans, 1984).

Chapter Four: Neuroscience and the Soul

1. Antonio R. Damasio, *Descartes' Error: Emotion, Reason, and the Human Brain* (New York: G.P. Putnam's Sons, 1994), 3-10.

2. Paul Churchland, *The Engine of Reason, the Seat of the Soul: A Philosophical Journey into the Brain* (Cambridge, Mass.: MIT Press, 1995), 159-60. This is a very accessible account of current brain research and includes philosophical treatment of important issues as well.

3. *Ibid.*, 179-80.

4. *Ibid.*, 159.

5. *Ibid.*, 157.

6. *Ibid.*, 179.

7. George Hunston Williams, *The Radical Reformation*, 3rd ed. (Kirksville, Mo.: Sixteenth Century Journal Publishers, 1992), 902.

Chapter Five: Christianity and Evolution

1. See, for example, Arthur Peacocke, *Theology for A Scientific Age*, 2nd ed. (Minneapolis: Fortress Press, 1993).

2. This is one of the reasons I emphasized in chapter three the *insufficiency* of the cosmological fine-tuning alone as grounds for an argument for the existence of God.

3. See Anne M. Clifford, "Darwin's Revolution in the *Origin of Species*: From Natural Theology to Natural Selection," in Robert J. Russell, William R. Stoeger, and Francisco J. Ayala, eds., *Biological Evolution: Scientific Perspectives on Divine Action* (Vatican City State and Berkeley, Calif.: Vatican Observatory and Center for Theology and the Natural Sciences, 1998).

4. See Francisco J. Ayala, "Darwin's Revolution," in John H. Campbell and J. William Schopf, eds., *Creative Evolution?!* (Boston and London: Jones and Bartlett Publishers, 1994), chap. 1.

5. See Thomas M. Ross, "The Implicit Theology of Carl Sagan," *Pacific Theological Review* 18 (1985) 3:24-32.

6. John Howard Yoder, "Binding and Loosing," in Michael G. Cartwright, ed., *The Royal Priesthood: Essays Ecclesiological and Ecumenical* (Grand Rapids, Mich.: Eerdmans, 1994), 325-358; quotation, 353.

7. Walter Wink, *Engaging the Powers* (Minneapolis: Fortress Press, 1992).

8. These discussions could all be clarified by distinguishing between the *capacity* for moral reasoning and the *content* of moral norms. Clearly the former evolved along with the rest of our intellectual abilities. But this does not imply that evolutionary theory explains the content of moral systems. See Francisco J. Ayala, "The Biological Roots of Morality," *Biology and Philosophy* (1987): 235-252.

9. Holmes Rolston, "Does Nature Need to be Redeemed?" *Zygon: Journal of Religion and Science,* 29, no. 2 (1994): 205-229; quotations 218-220.

10. Rollin Armour, *Anabaptist Baptism* (Scottdale, Pa.: Herald Press, 1966), 78; quoting Hans Hut, *Von dem geheimnus der tauf.*

11. Armour, 82.

12. John Howard Yoder, *The Politics of Jesus,* 2nd ed., (Grand Rapids, Mich.: Eerdmans, 1994), 246, 160.

13. For Yoder's reflection on the Prologue, see *He Came Preaching Peace* (Scottdale, Pa.: Herald Press, 1985), chap. 6.

14. James Wm. McClendon, Jr., *Ethics: Systematic Theology, Volume I* (Nashville, Tenn.: Abingdon Press, 1986), 147. McClendon's theology is written from the perspective of the Radical Reformation tradition. See also *Doctrine: Systematic Theology, Volume II* (Nashville, Tenn.: Abingdon Press, 1994).

15. John Wisdom, *Proceedings of the Aristotelian Society* (1944-45); reprinted in John Wisdom, *Philosophy and Psychoanalysis* (Oxford: Blackwell, 1953), 154-55.

Chapter Six: Radical Reformation Theology and Social Science

1. *The Legacy of Michael Sattler*, ed. John Howard Yoder (Scottdale, Pa.: Herald Press, 1973).

2. *Ibid.*, 74-75.

3. Bruno Latour, *We Have Never Been Modern*, trans. Catherine Porter, (Cambridge, Mass.: Harvard University Press, 1993), 33.

4. Max Weber, "Politics as Vocation," in *Politics as a Vocation* (Minneapolis: Fortress Press, 1965), 1.

5. Reinhold Niebuhr, *Moral Man and Immoral Society* (New York: Charles Scribner's Sons, 1932), xi-xii.

6. Peter Berger, *Invitation to Sociology: A Humanistic Perspective* (New York: Doubleday, 1963), 69.

7. Niebuhr, 257-58.

8. Account found in James W. Douglass, *The Non-Violent Cross: A Theology of Revolution and Peace* (Toronto, Ontario: The Macmillan Co. , 1966), 262-63.

9. See John Howard Yoder, *The Original Revolution: Essays on Christian Pacifism* (Scottdale, Pa.: Herald Press, 1971), chap. 3.

10. Jim Consedine, *Restorative Justice: Healing the Effects of Crime* (Lyttelton, N. Z. : Ploughshares Publications, 1995), 102.

11. *Ibid.*, 36.

12. *Ibid.*, 69, 67.

13. *Ibid.*, chap. 7.

14. For a more extensive argument regarding scientific evidence for the implementability of Jesus' social ethic, see Nancey Murphy and George F.R. Ellis, *On the Moral Nature of the Universe: Cosmology, Theology, and Ethics* (Minneapolis: Fortress Press, 1996). And for more extensive discussion of North American restorative justice, see Howard Zehr, *Changing Lenses: A New Focus for Crime and Justice* (Scottdale, Pa.: Herald Press, 1990, 1995).

15. For an argument to the effect that the radical tradition is more coherent than its Augustinian competitors, see Murphy and Ellis.

Index

About Pandora Press

Pandora Press is a small, independently owned press dedicated to making available modestly priced books that deal with Anabaptist, Mennonite, and Believers Church topics, both historical and theological. We welcome comments from our readers.

Later Writings by Pilgram Marpeck and his Circle. Volume 1: The Exposé, A Dialogue and Marpeck's Response to Caspar Schwenckfeld
> Translated by Walter Klaassen, Werner Packull, and John Rempel
> (Kitchener: Pandora Press, 1999; co-published with Herald Press)
> Softcover, 157pp. ISBN 0-9683462-6-X
> $20.00 U.S./$23.00 Canadian. Postage: $4.00 U.S./$5.00 Can.
> *[Previously untranslated writings by Marpeck and his Circle]*

John Driver, *Radical Faith. An Alternative History*
> *of the Christian Church*, edited by Carrie Snyder.
> (Kitchener: Pandora Press, 1999; co-published with Herald Press)
> Softcover, 334pp. ISBN 0-9683462-8-6
> $32.00 U.S./$35.00 Canadian. Postage: $5.00 U.S./$6.00 Can.
> *[A history of the church as it is seldom told – from the margins]*

C. Arnold Snyder, *From Anabaptist Seed.*
> *The Historical Core of Anabaptist-Related Identity*
> (Kitchener: Pandora Press, 1999; co-published with Herald Press)
> Softcover, 53pp.; discussion questions. ISBN 0-9685543-0-X
> $5.00 U.S./$6.25 Canadian. Postage: $2.00 U.S./$2.50 Can.
> *[Ideal for group study, commissioned by Mennonite World Conf.]*
> Also available in Spanish translation: *De Semilla Anabautista*, from Pandora Press only.

John D. Thiesen, *Mennonite and Nazi? Attitudes Among Mennonite Colonists in Latin America, 1933-1945.*
> (Kitchener: Pandora Press, 1999; co-published with Herald Press)
> Softcover, 330pp., 2 maps, 24 b/w illustrations, bibliography, index. ISBN 0-9683462-5-1
> $25.00 U.S./$28.00 Canadian. Postage: $4.00 U.S./$5.00 Can.
> *[Careful and objective study of an explosive topic]*

Lifting the Veil, a translation of *Aus meinem Leben: Erinnerungen von J.H. Janzen.* Ed. by Leonard Friesen; trans. by Walter Klaassen
> (Kitchener: Pandora Press, 1998; co-pub. with Herald Press).
> Softcover, 128pp.; 4pp. of illustrations. ISBN 0-9683462-1-9
> $12.50 U.S./$14.00 Canadian. Postage: $4.00 U.S. and Can.
> *[Memoir, confession, and critical observation of Mennonite life in Russia]*

Leonard Gross, *The Golden Years of the Hutterites*, rev. ed.
(Kitchener: Pandora Press, 1998; co-pub. with Herald Press).
Softcover, 280pp., index. ISBN 0-9683462-3-5
$22.00 U.S./$25.00 Canadian. Postage: $4.00 U.S./$5.00 Can.
[*Classic study of early Hutterite movement, now available again*]

The Believers Church: A Voluntary Church, ed. by William H. Brackney
(Kitchener: Pandora Press, 1998; co-published with Herald Press).
Softcover, viii, 237pp., index. ISBN 0-9683462-0-0
$25.00 U.S./$27.50 Canadian. Postage: $4.00 U.S./$5.00 Can.
[*Papers read at the 12th Believers Church Conference, Hamilton, Ont.*]

An Annotated Hutterite Bibliography, compiled by Maria H.
Krisztinkovich, ed. by Peter C. Erb (Kitchener, Ont.: Pandora Press,
1998). (Ca. 2,700 entries) 312pp., cerlox bound, electronic, or both.
ISBN (paper) 0-9698762-8-9/(disk) 0-9698762-9-7
$15.00 each, U.S. and Canadian. Postage: $6.00 U.S. and Can.
[*The most extensive bibliography on Hutterite literature available*]

Jacobus ten Doornkaat Koolman, *Dirk Philips. Friend and Colleague of
Menno Simons*, trans. W. E. Keeney, ed. C. A. Snyder
(Kitchener: Pandora Press, 1998; co-pub. with Herald Press).
Softcover, xviii, 236pp., index. ISBN: 0-9698762-3-8
$23.50 U.S./$28.50 Canadian. Postage: $4.00 U.S./$5.00 Can.
[*The definitive biography of Dirk Philips, now available in English*]

Sarah Dyck, ed./tr., *The Silence Echoes: Memoirs of Trauma & Tears*
(Kitchener: Pandora Press, 1997; co-published with Herald Press).
Softcover, xii, 236pp., 2 maps. ISBN: 0-9698762-7-0
$17.50 U.S./$19.50 Canadian. Postage: $4.00 U.S./$5.00 Can.
[*First person accounts of life in the Soviet Union, trans. from German*]

Wes Harrison, *Andreas Ehrenpreis and Hutterite Faith and Practice*
(Kitchener: Pandora Press, 1997; co-published with Herald Press).
Softcover, xxiv, 274pp., 2 maps, index. ISBN 0-9698762-6-2
$26.50 U.S./$32.00 Canadian. Postage: $4.00 U.S./$5.00 Can.
[*First biography of this important seventeenth century Hutterite leader*]

C. Arnold Snyder, *Anabaptist History and Theology: Revised Student
Edition* (Kitchener: Pandora Press, 1997; co-pub. Herald Press).
Softcover, xiv, 466pp., 7 maps, 28 illustrations, index, bibliography.
ISBN 0-9698762-5-4
$35.00 U.S./$38.00 Canadian. Postage: $5.00 U.S./$6.00 Can.
[*Abridged, rewritten edition for undergraduates and the non-specialist*]

Nancey Murphy, *Reconciling Theology and Science: A Radical Reformation Perspective* (Kitchener, Ont.: Pandora Press, 1997). Softcover, x, 103pp., index. ISBN 0-9698762-4-6 $14.50 U.S./$17.50 Canadian. Postage: $3.50 U.S./$4.00 Can.
[*Exploration of the supposed conflict between Christianity and Science*]

C. Arnold Snyder and Linda A. Huebert Hecht, eds, *Profiles of Anabaptist Women: Sixteenth Century Reforming Pioneers* (Waterloo, Ont.: Wilfrid Laurier University Press, 1996). Softcover, xxii, 442pp. ISBN: 0-88920-277-X $28.95 U.S. or Canadian. Postage: $5.00 U.S./$6.00 Can.
[*Biographical sketches of more than 50 Anabaptist women; a first*]

The Limits of Perfection: A Conversation with J. Lawrence Burkholder 2nd ed., with a new epilogue by J. Lawrence Burkholder, Rodney Sawatsky and Scott Holland, eds. (Kitchener: Pandora Press, 1996). Softcover, x, 154pp. ISBN 0-9698762-2-X $10.00 U.S./$13.00 Canadian. Postage: $2.00 U.S./$3.00 Can.
[*J.L. Burkholder on his life experiences; eight Mennonites respond*]

C. Arnold Snyder, *Anabaptist History and Theology: An Introduction* (Kitchener: Pandora Press, 1995). ISBN 0-9698762-0-3 Softcover, x, 434pp., 6 maps, 29 illustrations, index, bibliography. $35.00 U.S./$38.00 Canadian. Postage: $5.00 U.S./$6.00 Can.
[*Comprehensive survey; unabridged version, fully documented*]

C. Arnold Snyder, *The Life and Thought of Michael Sattler* (Scottdale: Herald Press, 1984). Hardcover, viii, 260pp. ISBN 0-8361-1264-4 $10.00 U.S./$12.00 Canadian. Postage: $4.00 U.S./$5.00 Can.
[*First full-length biography of this Anabaptist leader and martyr*]

Pandora Press
51 Pandora Avenue N.
Kitchener, Ontario
Canada N2H 3C1
Tel./Fax: (519) 578-2381
E-mail: panpress@golden.net
Web site: www.pandorapress.com

Herald Press
616 Walnut Avenue
Scottdale, PA
U.S.A. 15683
Orders: (800) 245-7894
E-mail: hp%mph@mcimail.com
Web site: www.mph.lm.com